THE FOREST AND THE TREES

THE FOREST AND THE TREES

Sociology as Life,

Practice,

and Promise

ALLAN G. JOHNSON

Temple University Press
Philadelphia

Temple University Press
Copyright © 1997 by Allan G. Johnson
All rights reserved
Published 1997
Printed in the United States of America

Interior design by Kate Nichols

♾ The paper used in this publication meets the
requirements of American National Standard for Information
Sciences—Permanence of Paper for Printed Library Materials, ANSI
Z39.48-1984

Library of Congress Cataloging-in-Publication Data
Johnson, Allan G.
The forest and the trees : sociology as life, practice, and
promise / Allan G. Johnson.
p.   cm.
Includes bibliographical references.
ISBN 1-56639-563-1 (cloth : alk. paper).
ISBN 1-56639-564-X (paper : alk. paper)
1. Sociology—Philosophy.   2. Sociology—Methodology.   I. Title.
HM26.J66   1997
301'.01—dc21   97-9093

For Alice

Contents

THE FOREST AND THE TREES

Introduction

I am a practicing sociologist. This book is about what it is that I practice and what it means and why it matters to practice it. This book is about how the practice finds its way into almost every aspect of life, from headlines in the morning paper to the experience of growing older to the ravages of social oppression in the world. It is about things small and things large, things simple and things complex well past what we can imagine.

I practice sociology in many ways. I practice it when I think about how social life works, when I write, when I work with people trying to see what's going on in the world and our lives in it. I practice as a consultant in corporations to help solve the dilemmas of a diverse and difficult world in which race, gender, sexual orientation, and other issues of difference cast dark shadows over people's lives. I practice when I walk down a street, shop in a market, or sit in a sidewalk restaurant, sip a cup of coffee, and watch the world go by and wonder what life *really* is all about, what this stream of interconnected people's lives consists of, what knits it all together and what tears it apart, and what, as my students would say, it's got to do with me.

I practice sociology for many reasons. I practice it because there is so much unnecessary suffering in the world, and to do something about it we need to understand where it comes from. In this sense, practicing sociology has a profoundly moral dimension. I don't mean this in the sense that it's about being good instead of bad. I mean it in a deeper and broader sense of morality that touches on the essence of what we're about as human beings and what our life together consists of. It is impossible to study social life for very long without coming up against the consequences that social life produces, and a lot of these consequences do such damage to people's lives that, unless we find ways to deny or ignore the reality of it, we feel compelled to ask "why?" And once we ask that question, we need tools to help make sense of where it leads and to imagine how we might go from there toward something better. We can't help but be part of the problem; practicing sociology is a way to also be part of the solution. This not only helps the world, but makes it easier to live in, especially given how crazy a place it can seem. It helps to be able to see how one thing is connected to another, and, in that, how to find ways to make some small difference. We can't change the world all by ourselves, but we can make informed decisions about how to participate in it, and how that can help turn the world toward something better, even if it's just in our neighborhoods or families or where we work.

I wouldn't do all this if I didn't believe something better was possible, so I have to add faith to my list of reasons for practicing sociology. I believe that the choices we make as individuals matter beyond our lives more than we can imagine, that things don't have to be the way they are, but that they won't get better all by themselves. We need to do something, and what we do needs to be based on more than hunches and personal opinion and prejudice. We need systematic ways to figure things out, and that's what sociological practice offers.

I also practice sociology because it helps to keep me in touch with the essence of my own life in the world, for sociology isn't simply about some larger world "out there." It's also about us in the world and the connection between the two, which means it can take us toward basic truths about who we are and what our lives are about. I practice it because it reminds me that for all that we think we know about things, beneath that is all that we don't know, which is good reason to feel awed from time to time. On some level, for example, I'm amazed that social life works at all, that we're able to live and work together as much as we do, to talk, dream, imagine, fight, and create. There is something miraculous about the simplest conversation, miraculous in the sense that there is a core truth about how it happens that we can never get to. We can contemplate the miracle of things by taking ourselves toward the limit of what we can know. And we can feel the fringe of core truths and how our lives are part of them. So, while my practice is usually "about" understanding the world, it is also about keeping myself in touch with the essentially unknowable essence of human existence that lies beneath.

Practicing sociology is a way to observe the world and to think about and make sense of it. It is a way to be in the world and *of* the world, to play a meaningful role in the life of our species as it shapes and reshapes itself into the mystery of what's going on and what it's got to do with us.

Practice What?

Most people probably have some notion of what I mean by "sociology," but I doubt that it looks much like sociology as it's practiced. If you've ever looked at a typical introductory sociology text (the only glimpse of sociology that most people ever have), for example, you probably see sociology as a collection of facts and terms about almost everything, from the family to economics to politics to crime to religion to the intricacies of conversation. It's like high school social studies, but at a "higher" level. But looking at all these varied aspects of social life isn't by itself sociological, because many disciplines look at these same areas. Criminal lawyers, legal scholars, and judges, for example, study crime; economists study economics; political scientists study politics; anthropologists, psychologists, historians, and divorce lawyers study families. But this doesn't mean they're practicing sociology.

This is why vague definitions of sociology as "about" groups and societies or "about" social life don't give us much that we can use. Since few words are as vague as "about," sociology winds up meaning pretty much whatever you want it to mean, which gets close to meaning nothing at all. This makes it easy to think that sociological practice is everywhere, that when *Time* or *Newsweek* or *MTV* or *Frontline* comments on something "social," they're doing sociology. It's also easy to think we can learn as much from reading the newspaper and watching television as we can by practicing sociology. As a result, many sociologists go out of their way to impress upon people that what they do is more than common sense. They're right, of course; it *is* much more than common sense (now I've done it, too), but having to convince people of it is a situation that sociologists have largely brought upon themselves. We keep digging a hole with one hand while trying to fill it in with the other.

You also won't find a clear sense of sociology by looking at scholarly journals. It's not that the authors aren't practicing sociology. It's that they're so far removed from caring to explain the *essence* of what they're doing that it gets buried beneath layers of data and theory, implicit rather than explicit. Since sociologists write primarily for one another, they seem to assume that the question of what sociology really amounts to isn't worth figuring out, much less articulating so that people outside the field can understand it. You could read several years worth of journal articles without getting a clue as to what it is that makes them sociological.

For some sociologists, the lack of a clear sense of sociology isn't a problem; it's just the nature of things. There is no one sociology, they argue, but instead a diversity of sociolo*gies*. It's futile, even presumptuous to look for a "grand narrative" that explains everything in one fell swoop. It's old-fashioned, rigid, and overly modernist; worse still, it won't work. It's undeniable that sociology encompasses a dazzling collection of ideas and methods and points of interest, and undoubtedly true that no theory can explain everything. But if the nature of things is that sociology revolves around many different "narratives," *we still have to ask ourselves what it is about these narratives that justifies calling them all "sociological."* If we can't answer that in a reasonably clear and straightforward way, then it's hard to see why anyone would take sociological practice seriously. And without that, without some way for people to grasp the defining essence of what sociologists do and why they do it, all the research and theory in the world won't amount to much except for sociologists.

That is why I've written this book. The premise for *The Forest and the Trees* is a hypothetical situation I put myself in when I started writing it. If sociology could teach everyone just *one* thing, if it could pass along just one central insight, what would that be? Would it be something about the family? About political institutions? About social inequality? About the use of language in social interaction? About conflict theory, exchange theory, functionalism, postmodernism, or any of the other theoretical perspectives sociologists have used over the years? Would it, in short, be some piece of data or a term or a theory from the mountain of data, terms, and theories that fall under the general rubric of sociology? I don't think so; or, at least, I hope not. Far simpler and more powerful would be a core idea that serves as a starting point, a gateway opening on questions that in turn point toward everything else. By itself, it wouldn't explain anything; that wouldn't be the point of it. Instead, it would define a core view of reality on which sociological practice of all kinds is based, consciously or not. And, in that, it would provide a touchstone for what it means to do sociology.

When I say that I practice sociology, I refer to that core view, that common ground that joins so many kinds of work. This book is one practicing sociologist's answer to the hypothetical, the core insight with the greatest potential to transform how people see the world and themselves in it. This book is about what that core view is and why it matters that we understand it, use it, live it, and pass it on.

1

The Forest, the Trees, and
the One Thing

As a form of sociological practice, I work with people in corporations, schools, and universities who are trying to deal with issues of diversity. In the simplest sense, diversity is about the variety of people in the world, the varied mix of gender, race, age, social class, ethnicity, religion, and other social characteristics.[1] In the United States and Europe, for example, the workforce is changing as the percentages who are female or from non-European ethnic and racial backgrounds increase and the percentage who are white and male declines.

If the changing mix was all that diversity amounted to, there wouldn't be a problem since in many ways differences make life interesting and enhance creativity. Compared with homogeneous teams, for example, diverse work teams are usually better with problems that require creative solutions. To be sure, diversity brings with it difficulties to be dealt with such as language barriers and different ways of doing things that can confuse or irritate people. But we're the species with the "big brain," the adaptable ones who learn quickly, so learning to get along with people unlike ourselves shouldn't be a problem we can't handle. Like travelers in a strange land, we'd simply learn about one another and make room for differences and figure out how to make good use of them.

As most people know, however, in the world as it is, difference amounts to more than just variety. It's also used as a basis for including some and excluding others, for rewarding some more and others less, for treating some with respect and dignity and some as if they were less than fully human or not even there. Difference is used as a basis for privilege, from reserving for some the simple human dignities that everyone should have, to the extreme of deciding who lives and who dies.[2] Since the workplace is part of the world, patterns of inequality and oppression that permeate the world also show up at work, even though people may like to think of themselves as "colleagues" or part of "the team." And just as these patterns shape people's lives in often damaging ways, they can eat away at the core of a community or an organization, weakening it with internal division and resentment bred and fed by injustice and suffering.

Some organizations realize the importance of a workplace where everyone feels accepted and valued for who they are and what they can contribute. One way to bring this about is to run programs to help people see what's going on, the consequences it produces, how these consequences affect people in different ways, and what they can do about it to create something better. The hardest thing about this work is that people are so reluctant to talk about privilege, especially those who belong to privileged groups. When the subject of race and racism comes up, white people often withdraw into silence as if paralyzed by guilt or other feelings they don't dare express. Or they push back, angry and defensive, as if they were being personally attacked and blamed for something they didn't do. Men often react similarly to issues of gender and sexism.

Because members of privileged groups often react negatively to looking at privilege, women, blacks, Latinos, gays, lesbians, workers, and other groups may not bring it up. They know how easily privilege can be used to retaliate against them for challenging the status quo and making people feel uncomfortable. So, rather than look at the reality of what's going on, the typical pattern in organizations—and just about everywhere else—is to choose between two equally futile alternatives: to be stuck in cycles of guilt, blame, and defensiveness; or to avoid talking about issues of privilege at all. Either way, the old destructive patterns and their consequences for people's lives continue.

Why does this happen? A major reason is that people tend to think of things only in terms of individuals, as if a society or a company or a university were nothing more than a collection of people living in a particular time and place. Many writers have pointed out how individualism affects social life. It isolates us from one another, promotes divisive competition, and makes it harder to sustain a sense of community, of all being "in this together." But individualism does more than affect how we participate in social life. It also affects how we *think* about social life and how we make sense of it. If we think everything begins and ends with individuals—their personalities, biographies, feelings, and behavior—then it's easy to think that social problems must come down to flaws in individual character. If we have a drug problem, it must be because individuals just can't or won't "say no." If there is racism, sexism, heterosexism, classism, and other forms of oppression, it must be because of people who for some reason have the personal "need" to behave in racist, sexist, and other oppressive ways. If evil consequences occur in social life, then it must be because of evil people and their evil ways and motives.

If we think about the world in this way—which is especially common in the United States—then it's easy to see why members of privileged groups get upset when they're asked to look at the benefits that go with belonging to that particular group and the price others pay for it. When women, for example, talk about how sexism affects them, individualistic thinking encourages men to hear this as a personal accusation: "If women are oppressed, then I'm an evil oppressor who wants to oppress them." Since no man wants to see himself as a bad person, and since most men probably don't *feel* oppressive toward women, men may feel unfairly attacked.

In the United States, individualism goes back to the nineteenth century and, beyond that, to the European Enlightenment and the certainties of modernist thinking. It was in this period that the rational mind of the individual person was recognized and elevated to a dominant position in the hierarchy of things, separated from and placed above even religion and God. The roots of individualistic thinking in the United States trace in part to the work of William James who helped pioneer the field of psychology. Later, it was deepened in Europe and the United States by Sigmund Freud's revolutionary insights into the existence of the subconscious and the inner world of individual existence. Over the course of the twentieth century, the individual life has emerged as a dominant framework for understanding the complexities and mysteries of human existence.

You can see this in bookstores and best-seller lists that abound with promises to change the world through "self-help" and individual growth and transformation. Even on the grand scale of societies—from war and politics to international economics—individualism reduces everything to the personalities and behavior of the people we perceive to be "in charge." If ordinary people in capitalist societies feel deprived and insecure, the individualistic answer is that the people who run corporations are "greedy" or the politicians are corrupt and incompetent and otherwise lacking in personal character. The same perspective argues that poverty exists because of the habits, attitudes, and skills of individual poor people, who are blamed for what they supposedly lack as people and told to change if they want anything better for themselves. To make a better world, we think we have to put the "right people" in charge or make better people by liberating human consciousness in a New Age or by changing how children are socialized or by locking up or tossing out or killing people who won't or can't be better than they are. Psychotherapy is increasingly offered as a model for changing not only the inner life of individuals, but also the world they live in. If enough people heal themselves through therapy, then the world will "heal" itself as well. The solution to collective problems such as poverty or deteriorating cities then becomes a matter not of collective solutions but of an accumulation of individual solutions. So, if we want to have less poverty in the world, the answer lies in raising people out of poverty or keeping them from becoming poor, *one person at a time.*

So, individualism is a way of thinking that encourages us to explain the world in terms of what goes on inside individuals and nothing else. We've been able to think this way because we've developed the human ability to be reflexive, which is to say, we've learned to look at ourselves *as selves* with greater awareness and insight than before. We can think about what kind of people we are and how we live in the world, and we can imagine ourselves in new ways. To do this, however, we first have to be able to believe that we exist as distinct individuals apart from the groups and communities and societies that make up our social environment. In other words, the *idea* of the "individual" has to exist before we think about ourselves as individuals, and the idea of the individual has been around for only a few centuries. Today, we've gone far beyond this by thinking of the social environment itself as just a collection of individuals: Society *is* people and people *are* society. To understand social life, all we have to do is understand what makes the individual psyche tick.

If you grow up and live in a society that's dominated by individualism, the idea that society is just people seems obvious. The problem is that this approach ignores the difference between the individual people who participate in social life and the relationships that connect them to one another and to groups and societies. It's true that you can't have a social relationship without people to participate in it and make it happen, but the people and the relationship aren't the same thing. That's why this book's title plays on the old saying about missing the forest for the trees. In one sense, a forest is simply a collection of individual trees; but it's more than that. It's also a collection of trees that exist *in a particular relation* to one another, and you can't tell what that relation is by just looking at each individual tree. Take a thousand trees and scatter them across the Great Plains of North America, and all you have are a thousand trees. But take those same trees and bring them close together and you have a forest. Same individual trees, but in one case a forest and in another case just a lot of trees.

The "empty space" that separates individual trees from one another isn't a characteristic of any one tree or the characteristics of all the individual trees somehow added together. It's something more than that, and it's crucial to understand the *relationships among* trees that make a forest what it is. Paying attention to that "something more"—whether it's a family or a corporation or an entire society—and how people are related to it is at the heart of sociological practice.

The One Thing

If sociology could teach everyone just one thing with the best chance to lead toward everything else we could know about social life, it would, I believe, be this: *We are always participating in something larger than ourselves, and if we want to understand social life and what happens to people in it, we have to understand what it is that we're participating in* and *how we participate in it.* In other words, the key to understanding social life isn't just the forest and it isn't just the trees. It's the forest *and* the trees and how they're related to one another. Sociology is the study of how all this happens.

The "larger" things we participate in are called social systems, and they come in all shapes and sizes. In general, the concept of a system refers to any collection of parts or elements that are connected in ways that cohere into some kind of whole. We can think of the engine in a car as a system, for example, a collection of parts arranged in ways that make the car "go." Or we could think of a language as a system, with words and punctuation and rules for how to combine them into sentences that mean something. We can also think of a family as a system—a collection of elements related to one another in a way that leads us to think of it as a unit. These include things such as the positions of mother, father, wife, husband, parent, child, daughter, son, sister, and brother. Elements also include shared ideas that tie those positions together to make relationships, such as how "good mothers" are supposed to act in relation to children or what a "family" is and what makes family members "related" to one another as kin. If we take the positions and the ideas and other elements, then we can think of what results as a whole and call it a social system.

In similar ways, we can think of corporations or societies as social systems. They differ from one another—and from families—in the kinds of elements they include and how those are arranged in relation to one another. Corporations have positions such as CEOs and stockholders, for example; but the position of "mother" isn't part of the corporate system. People who work in corporations can certainly be mothers in families, but that isn't a position that connects them to a corporation. Such differences are a key to seeing how systems work and produce different kinds of consequences. Corporations are sometimes referred to as "families," for example, but if you look at how families and corporations are actually put together as systems, it's easy to see how unrealistic such notions are. Families don't usually "lay off" their members when times are tough or to boost the bottom line, and they usually don't divide the food on the dinner table according to who's the strongest and best able to grab the lion's share for themselves.[3] But corporations dispense with workers all the time as a way to raise dividends and the value of stock, and top managers routinely take a huge share of each year's profits even while putting other members of the corporate "family" out of work.

What social life comes down to, then, is social systems and how people participate in and relate to them. Note that people *participate* in systems without being *parts* of the systems themselves. In this sense, "father" is a position in my family, and I, Allan, am a person who actually occupies that position. It's a crucial distinction that's easy to lose sight of. It's easy to lose sight of because we're so used to thinking solely in terms of individuals. It's crucial because it means that people aren't systems, and systems aren't people, and if we forget that, we're likely to focus on the wrong thing in trying to solve our problems.

Thinking of systems as just people is why members of privileged groups often take it personally when someone points out that society is racist or sexist or classist. "The United States is a racist society that privileges whites over other racial groups" is a statement that describes the United States as a social system. It does *not* thereby describe me or anyone else as an individual, for that has more to do with how each of us participates in society. As an individual, I can't avoid participating and can't help but be affected and shaped by that. But how all that plays out in practice depends on many things, including the choices I make about *how* to participate. Born in 1946, I grew up listening to the radio shows of the day, including *Amos and Andy* which was full of racist stereotypes about blacks (the actors were white). Like any other child, I looked to my environment to define what was "funny." Since this show was clearly defined as "funny" from a white perspective in a white society, and since I was born white,

I laughed along with everyone else as we drove down the highway listening to the car radio. I even learned to "do" the voices
of "black" characters and regaled my family with renditions of
classic lines from the show.

More than forty years later, those racist images are firmly
lodged in my memory; once they get in, there's no way to get
them out. With the benefit of hindsight, I see the racism in them
and how they're connected to massive injustice and suffering in
the society I participate in. As an individual, I can't undo the past
and I can't undo my childhood. I can, however, choose what to do
about race and racism *now*. I can't make my society or the place
where I live or work suddenly nonracist, but I can decide how to
live as a white person in relation to my privileged *position* as a
white person. I can decide whether to laugh or object when I hear
racist "humor"; I can decide how to treat people who aren't clas-
sified as "white"; I can decide what to do about the consequences
that racism produces for people, whether to be part of the solution or merely part of the problem. I don't feel guilty because my
country is racist, because that wasn't my doing. But as a white
person who *participates* in that society, I feel responsible to consider what to do about it. The only way to get past the potential
for guilt and see how I can make a difference is to realize that the
system isn't me and I'm not the system.

Nonetheless, systems and people are closely connected to
each other, and seeing how that works is a basic part of sociological practice. One way to see this is to compare social systems to
a game such as Monopoly. We can think of Monopoly as a social
system. It has positions (players, banker); it has a material reality (the board, the pieces, the dice, play money, property deeds,
houses and hotels); and it has ideas that connect all of this to-

gether in a set of relationships. There are values that define the point of the game—to win—and rules that spell out what's allowed in pursuit of winning, including the idea of cheating. Notice that we can describe the game without saying anything about the personalities, intentions, attitudes, or other characteristics of the people who might play it. The game, in other words, has an existence that we can describe all by itself. "It" exists whether or not anyone is playing it at the moment. The same is true of social systems. We don't have to describe actual basketball players in order to describe "a basketball team" as a kind of system that has characteristics that distinguish it from other systems.

I don't play Monopoly anymore, mostly because I don't like the way I behave when I do. When I used to play Monopoly, I'd try to win, even against my own children, and I couldn't resist feeling good when I did (we're *supposed* to feel good) even if I also felt guilty about it. Why did I act and feel this way? It wasn't because I have a greedy, mercenary personality, because I know that I don't behave this way when I'm not playing Monopoly. Clearly I am *capable* of behaving this way as an individual, which is part of the explanation. But the rest of it comes down to the simple fact that I behaved that way because winning is what *Monopoly* is about. When I participate in that system, greedy behavior is presented to me as a path of least resistance. As defined by the game, it's what you're supposed to do; it's the point. And when I play the game, I feel obliged to go by its rules and pursue the values it promotes. I look upon the game as having some kind of authority over the people who play it, which becomes apparent when I consider how rare it is for people to suggest changing the rules ("I'm sorry, honey," I say as I take my kid's last dollar, "but that's just the way the game is played"). If *we* were the game, then we'd feel free to play by any rules we liked. But we tend not to see games—or systems—in that way. We tend to see them as external to us and therefore not ours to shape however we please.

What happens when people participate in a social system depends on two things: the system and how it works, and what people actually do as they participate in it from one moment to the next. What people do depends on who they are in relation to the system and other people in it (in Monopoly, everyone occupies the same position—player—but in a classroom there are teachers and students and in a corporation there can be hundreds of different positions). People are what make a system "happen." Without their participation, a system exists only as an idea with some physical reality attached. If no one plays Monopoly, it's just a bunch of stuff in a box with rules written inside the cover. And if no one plays "Ford Motor Company," it's just a bunch of factories and offices and equipment and rules and accounts written on paper and stored in computers. In a similar sense, a society may be "racist" or "sexist," but for racism or sexism to actually happen—or not—someone has to do or not do something in relation to someone else.

For its part, a system affects how we think, feel, and behave as participants. It does this by laying out paths of least resistance. At any given moment, there are an almost infinite number of possible things we could do, but we typically don't realize that and see only a narrow range of possibilities. What the range looks like depends on the system we're in. While playing Monopoly, I *could* reach over and take money from the bank whenever I wanted, but I probably wouldn't like the reaction I'd get from other players. When someone I like lands on a property I own, I *could* tell them that I'll give them a break and not collect the rent, but then collect it happily when someone I don't like lands there. But people would probably object that I wasn't playing "fair" or by the rules. Since I'd rather people not be angry at me or kick me out of the game, it's easier to go by the rules even when I'd rather not. And so I usually do, following the path of least resistance that's presented to people who occupy my position in that particular system. This is why people might laugh at racist or sexist jokes even when it makes them feel uncomfortable—because in that situation, to not laugh and risk being ostracized by everyone may make them feel *more* uncomfortable. The easiest—although not necessarily easy—choice is to go along. This doesn't mean we *will* go along, only that if we go along we'll run into less resistance than if we don't.

In other situations, paths of least resistance might look quite different, and giving a friend a break or objecting to sexist humor might be seen as just what we're supposed to do. In relation to my children, for example, I'm supposed to do whatever I can to help them—that's the path of least resistance that goes with the relation between parent and child in the family system (except, perhaps, when we're playing Monopoly). This is why I'd never want my daughter or son as a student in one of my classes, because I'd have to choose between conflicting paths of least resistance associated with two different systems. As a teacher, I'm supposed to treat my students the same; but, as a father, I'm supposed to treat my children as my "favorites" above other people's children. The path of least resistance in one system is a path of much greater resistance in the other; hence the dilemma posed by what sociologists call "role conflict."[4]

So, social systems and people are connected through a dynamic relationship. People make systems happen, and systems lay out paths of least resistance that shape how people participate. Neither exists without the other, and yet neither can simply be reduced to the other. My life isn't simply a predictable product of the systems I participate in; and social systems aren't simply an accumulation of my own and other people's lives. What results from all this is the patterns of social life and the consequences they produce for people, for systems themselves, and for the world—in short, most of what matters in the human scheme of things.

On the surface, the idea that we're always participating in something larger than ourselves may seem fairly simple. But like many ideas that seem simple at first, it can take us places that transform how we look at the world and ourselves in it.

Individualistic Models Don't Work

Probably the most important basis for sociological practice is to realize that *the individualistic perspective that dominates current thinking about social life doesn't work*. Nothing we do or experience takes place in a vacuum; everything is always related to a context of some kind. When a wife and husband argue about who'll clean the bathroom, for example, or who'll take care of a sick child when they both work outside the home, the issue is never simply about the two of them even though it may seem that way at the time. We have to ask about the larger context in which this takes place. We might ask how this instance is related to living in a society organized in ways that privilege men over women, in part by not making men feel obliged to share equally in domestic work except when they choose to "help out." On an individual level, he may think she's being a nag; she may think he's being a jerk; but it's never as simple as that. What both may miss is that in a different kind of society, they might not be having this argument in the first place because both might feel obliged to take care of the home and children. In similar ways, when we see ourselves as a unique result of the family we came from, we overlook how each family is connected to larger patterns. The emotional problems we struggle with as individuals aren't due simply to what kind of parents we had, for their participation in social systems—at work, in the community, in society as a whole—shaped them as people, including their roles as mothers and fathers.

An individualistic model is misleading because it encourages us to explain human behavior and experience from a perspective that's so narrow it misses most of what's going on. A related problem is that *we can't understand what goes on in social systems simply by looking at individuals.* In one sense, for example, suicide is a solitary act done by an individual, typically while alone.[5] If we ask why people kill themselves, we're likely to think first of how people feel when they do it—hopeless, depressed, guilty, lonely, or perhaps obliged by honor or duty to sacrifice themselves for someone else or some greater social good. That might explain suicides taken one at a time, but what do we have when we add up all the suicides that happen in a society for a given year? What does that number tell us, and, more importantly, about what? The suicide rate for the entire U.S. population in 1994, for example, was twelve suicides per 100,000 people. If we look inside that number, we find that the rate for males was twenty per 100,000, but the rate for females was only five per 100,000. The rate also differs dramatically by race and country and varies over time. The suicide rate for white males, for example, was 71 percent higher than for black males, and the rate for white females was more than twice that for black females. While the rate in the United States was twelve per 100,000, it was thirty-four per 100,000 in Hungary and only seven per 100,000 in Italy. So, in the United States, males and whites are far more likely than females and blacks to kill themselves; and people in the United States are almost twice as likely as Italians to commit suicide but only one third as likely as Hungarians.[6]

If we use an individualistic model to explain such differences, we'll tend to see them as nothing more than a sum of individual suicides. If males are more likely to kill themselves, then it must be because males are more likely to feel suicidally depressed, lonely, worthless, and hopeless. In other words, the psychological factors that cause individuals to kill themselves must be more common among U.S. males than they are among U.S. females, or more common among people in the United States than among Italians. There's nothing wrong with such reasoning; it may be exactly right *as far as it goes*. But that's just the problem: It doesn't go very far because it doesn't answer the question of *why* these differences exist in the first place. Why, for example, would males be more likely to feel suicidally hopeless and depressed than females, or Hungarians more likely than Italians? Or why would Hungarians who feel suicidally depressed be more likely to go ahead and kill themselves than Italians who feel the same way? To answer such questions, we need more than an understanding of individual psychology. Among other things, we need to pay attention to the fact that words like "female," "white," and "Italian" name positions that people occupy in social systems. This draws attention to how those systems work and what it means to occupy those positions in them.

Sociologically, a suicide rate is a number that describes something about a group or a society, not the individuals who belong to it. A suicide rate of twelve per 100,000 tells us nothing about you or me or anyone else. Each of us either commits suicide during a given year or we don't, and the rate can't tell us who does what. In the same way, how individuals feel before they kill themselves isn't by itself enough to explain why some groups or societies have higher suicide rates than others. Individuals can feel depressed or lonely, but groups and societies can't feel a thing. We could consider that Italians might tend to be less depressed than people in the United States, for example, or that in the United States, people might tend to deal with feelings of depression more effectively than Hungarians. It makes no sense at all, however, to say that the United States is more depressed or lonely than Italy.

While it might work to look at what goes on in individuals as a way to explain why one person commits suicide, this can't explain *patterns* of suicide found in social systems. To do this, we have to look at how people feel and behave *in relation to* systems and how these systems work. We need to ask, for example, how societies are organized in ways that encourage people who participate in them to feel more or less depressed or to respond to such feelings in suicidal or nonsuicidal ways. We need to see how belonging to particular groups shapes people's experience as they participate in social life, and how this limits the alternatives they think they can choose from. What is it about being male or being white that can make suicide a path of least resistance? How, in other words, can we go to the heart of sociological practice to ask how people participate in something larger than themselves and see how this affects the choices they make? How can we see the relationship between people and systems that produces variations in suicide rates or, for that matter, just about everything else that we do and experience, from having sex to going to school to working to dying?

Just as we can't tell what's going on in a system just by looking at individuals, we also can't tell what's going on in individuals just by looking at systems. Something may look like one thing in the system as a whole, but something else entirely when we look at the people who participate in it. If we look at the kind of mass destruction and suffering that war typically causes, for example, an individualistic model suggests a direct link with the "kinds" of people who participate in it. If war produces cruelty, bloodshed, aggression, and conquest, then it must be that the people who participate in it are cruel, bloodthirsty, aggressive people who want to conquer and dominate others. Viewing the carnage and destruction that war typically leaves in its wake, we're likely to ask, "What kind of people could do such a thing?" Sociologically, however, this question misleads us by reducing a social phenomenon to a simple matter of "kinds of people" without looking at the systems those people participate in. Since we're always participating in one system or another, when someone drops a bomb that incinerates thousands of people, we can't explain what happened simply by figuring out "what kind of person would do such a thing." In fact, if we look at what's known about people who fight in wars, they appear fairly normal by most standards and anything but bloodthirsty and cruel. Most accounts portray men in combat, for example, as alternating between boredom and feeling scared out of their wits. They worry much less about glory than they do about not being hurt or killed and getting themselves and their friends home in one piece. For most soldiers, killing and the almost constant danger of being killed are traumatic experiences that leave them forever changed as people. They go to war not in response to some inner need to be aggressive and kill, but because they think it's their duty to go, because they'll go to prison if they dodge the draft, because they've seen war portrayed in books and movies as an adventurous way to prove they're "real men," or because they don't want to risk family and friends rejecting them for not measuring up as true patriots.

People aren't systems, and systems aren't people, which means that social life can produce horrible or wonderful consequences without necessarily meaning that the people who participate in them are horrible or wonderful. Good people participate in systems that produce bad consequences all the time. I'm often aware of this in the simplest situations, such as when I go to buy clothes or food. Many of the clothes sold in the United States are made in sweatshops in cities like Los Angeles and New York and in Third World countries, where people work under conditions that resemble slavery in many respects, and for wages that are so low they can barely live on them. A great deal of the fruit and vegetables in stores are harvested by migrant farm workers who work under conditions that aren't much better. If these workers were provided with decent working conditions and paid a living wage, the price of clothing and food would probably be a lot higher than it is. This means that I benefit directly from the daily mistreatment and exploitation of thousands of people. The fact that I benefit doesn't make me a bad person; but my participation in that system does involve me in what happens to them.

It's About Us and
It's Not About Us

If we start from the idea that we're always participating in something larger than ourselves and that social life flows from this relationship, then we have to consider that we're all involved—even if only indirectly—in the social consequences that result, both the good and the bad. By definition, if I participate in a racist society— no matter what my race—then I'm involved in white privilege and racist consequences. As an individual, I may not feel or act in racist ways and in my heart I may even hate racism; but that's beside the core sociological point. I'm *involved* in one way or another by virtue of my participation in society itself.[7] If someone takes what I say more seriously because I'm white, then I've received a benefit of racism whether I'm aware of it or not, and in doing so, I've unwittingly participated in racism. This raises the question of how society works *and* how I participate in it—whether I actively defend white privilege or let people know I'm against racism or just go about my business and pretend there's no problem to begin with.

In diversity training sessions, this simple insight can dramatically alter how people see potentially painful issues and themselves in relation to them. This is especially true for people in privileged groups who otherwise resist looking at the nature and consequences of privilege. Their defensive resistance is probably the biggest single barrier to ending racism, sexism, and other forms of social oppression. Most of the time it happens because, like everyone else, they're stuck in an individualistic model of the world and can't see a way to acknowledge racial privilege as a fact of social life without also feeling personally blamed and guilty for it. And the people who are most likely to feel this way are often the ones who are otherwise most open to doing something to make things better. When they look at a problem like racism sociologically, however, they can see how it's both about them and not about them. It's not about them in the sense that they didn't create the racist society we all live in. As I was growing up white, no one asked me if it was OK with me for white people to use *Amos and Andy* to make fun of black people and keep them in their place beneath white privilege. And if they *had* asked me, I doubt that as a child I'd have known enough to object. In this sense, white people who've grown up in a racist environment have no reason to feel guilty when they hear anger about the existence of white racism and the harm and suffering it causes.

Racism *is* about me personally, however, because whether or not I'm conscious of it, I'm always making choices about how to participate in a society that is organized in racist ways and that makes behavior that perpetuates white privilege a path of least resistance. Regardless of how I behave, as a white person I have privileges that are at the expense of people of other races. Race privilege is built into the system itself, which means I don't have to like it or believe in it or even do anything to receive it. When I go shopping at the mall, sales people and store detectives don't follow me around as if I was going to steal something. They don't swoop down on me and pointedly ask "Can I help you?" as if I was a suspicious character or something other than a serious customer. But black people are mistreated this way all the time, and it usually doesn't matter how well they dress or how much money they have to spend.[8] Most people would agree that everyone should be treated decently, but when some are and some aren't simply because of which group they belong to, then social privilege is at work. And whether I like it or not, as a white person I benefit from that by getting something of value that's denied to them. Once I see this, it's hard to avoid asking about how I participate in the system that produces such racist consequences. What are my responsibilities? What could I do differently that would contribute to different outcomes? How can I be part of the solution to racism rather than merely part of the problem?

In other words, by making me aware that I'm involved in something larger than myself, sociological practice gets me off the hook of personal guilt and blame for a world that I didn't create and that isn't my fault. At the same time, however, it makes me aware of how I choose to participate in that world and how and why that matters. I have no reason to feel guilty simply because I'm white; but I also don't have the luxury of thinking that racism and race privilege have nothing to do with me.[9]

Personal Solutions Can't Solve Social Problems

If the shape of social life is rooted in both people *and* the systems they participate in, then this is also where change has to happen. Personal solutions are just that—personal and individual—and they cannot solve social problems unless they extend outward to connect with systems. An individualistic model encourages us to think that if enough individuals change, then systems will change as well, but a sociological perspective shows why change isn't this simple. The problem is that social life isn't simply a product of people's personal characteristics and behavior, for *these* arise out of their participation in social systems. In that sense, social life depends on how people are connected to one another through social relationships, and systems don't change unless relationships change.

An individualistic model also doesn't work because personal solutions arise primarily from a sense of our own personal needs, and focusing our attention on this is a path of least resistance. Once we find a solution to the problem that works for us personally, we've accomplished our goal and are likely to leave the problem behind rather than stay with it to help make things better for others. In the United States, for example, personal solutions are the typical response to the problem of economic insecurity. Insecurity seems to be a way of life for the vast majority of people in most capitalist societies. Rather than stop and ask how the system itself sets us up to feel insecure, we instead work hard to establish our own private zones of safety within an insecure system. The easiest thing for people to do then is to hang on to what they've got and leave everyone else to fend for themselves. Not surprisingly, this doesn't lower the overall level of insecurity and poverty in society as a whole; it doesn't, in other words, solve these *social* problems. Instead, it shuffles people in and out of various levels of well-being and security, like a game of musical chairs. As long as I've got a chair for me, why raise questions about the fact that there aren't enough chairs for everyone?

Sociological practice uses more complex models of change

that focus on several different levels of social life at once. Consider, for example, the problem of pollution, which a growing number of communities around the world are having to deal with. Suppose that people in your town start getting sick. Large numbers of children don't show up for school and local clinics and hospital emergency rooms are jammed with patients. The doctors figure out that people are suffering from chemical toxins.

On a purely individual level, we could say that we've figured out why people are getting sick. And to solve the problem in terms of individuals, we could just treat each sick person until they're well and change people's behavior so that they don't get sick again. If the chemicals are in the water supply, then don't drink the water. Buy bottled water instead. Each person now has a solution to the problem, if they can afford to drink bottled water or, perhaps, install expensive filtration systems in their houses. It would probably turn out that, like most communities, some would be able to afford this individualist solution and some wouldn't, which means that some people would still get sick. Of course we might enact some kind of collective response to this inequality by providing subsidies for poor people to buy bottled water, but notice that we still wouldn't have done anything about the underlying problem of polluted water. We would simply have found a way for individual people to avoid drinking it.

To take the problem to a sociological level, we have to ask about systems and how people participate in them, and so far we haven't said anything about people getting sick as a systemic problem. People are told to change how they participate in the system—don't drink water out of the tap. But nothing's been said about the possibility of changing the system they're participating in. Suppose we trace the toxin backwards from each faucet and wind up at the local reservoir. From there, we trace it to the surrounding earth and a stream, and from there to a local chemical plant that employs a large number of people in the town. Now we have a different explanation of why people are getting sick and a different solution: get the plant to stop dumping chemical wastes in ways that wind up in the town's water supply.

Suppose, however, that the people who run the company say they can't do that because it would cost too much, and the business they're in is so competitive that they'd have to close down the plant and move to where people care more about their jobs than they do about polluted water. And if the owners close down the plant, a lot of local people will lose their jobs, the effects of which will ripple out through the town as fewer people have money to spend in local business or pay in local taxes to support schools and such. Now the problem of what's making people sick is more than simply a matter of how the plant is run. It's also related to still larger systems that the plant as a whole participates in and the company's powerful position in relation to the community that depends on it for jobs. The nature of the economic system—competitive global capitalism—shapes the choices that plant owners make in ways that affect the quality of water that people have to drink. That economic system is tied to values about the desirability of making a profit and the right of people to do what they want with private property, perhaps even including dumping toxic wastes on land they "own" or in streams that run across their property. Ultimately, the town may have to confront the company's power over their lives and choose between powerful competing values about how entire societies are organized.

Taking the problem to the level of systems doesn't mean we have to ignore individuals. It isn't a matter of one or the other, because sociological practice looks at social life in relation to systems *and* how people participate in them. People often box themselves into a false choice between attributing a problem to "society" or blaming it on individuals. But social life doesn't work that way. It's hardly ever a matter of simply one or the other, of society *or* individuals, because societies and individuals always exist in relation to each other. The challenge of sociological practice is to see how this works. If we don't, we go back and forth between acting as if individuals play no part in creating social problems or acting as if people behave in a social vacuum without being affected by the kind of society they live in. There is a third alternative: It's a matter of both/and, not either/or. Systems don't change without people changing at one point or another; and no system can change through individual change alone.

It's Messier and
More Interesting than That

The language of "systems" and "individuals" can make things seem a lot simpler and clear-cut than they really are. It encourages us to think of systems as things, as rigid molds that people must fit into. In some ways a social system is "thing-like" in that we can identify characteristics such as rules or a physical setting or positions that people occupy when they participate in it. "School," for example, conjures up some predictable images—of rooms with chairs in rows, chalk boards, cafeterias, gymnasiums, libraries, computers, students, teachers, locker-lined hallways, bells ringing at regular intervals, rules, grades, semesters, vacations, teaching, learning, graduation. Because such images of this thing we call school are relatively fixed in our minds, we can experience it as being thing-like in some ways. In other words, we can think of it as something outside of us, as an "it" rather than a "me" or even an "us." People attend or work in "it," but the people aren't it and it isn't them. In that way, school is like the game of Monopoly in a box. People take it out (go to school), play it for awhile (teach, study, administer), and then put it away (go home). And that's pretty much what it is, or so we might think.

But social life is messier and more interesting than that, because in many ways social systems aren't some*thing*. They are an ongoing process. They are continually being created and recreated as people *do* things in order to make them *happen*. The associations we have with school are just words on a page, images in our minds, until people actually participate in the process of school as a system. When they do, some familiar patterns shape what goes on, but there is also an enormous amount of variation around those patterns as people put their own spin on how they're going to participate. "It" never happens just the same way twice, because what we call "school" is as much about what people do as it is about all the associations we have with the idea of school as a social system. While we may not be aware of it at the time, at any given moment any of the people in school could do something unexpected that would shape how school happens in that time and place. We may have a general understanding of what school is in the same way that we understand what Monopoly is. And we can use such knowledge to predict with some accuracy what the general patterns will look like in a given school on a given day. But there is a great deal that we can't predict because in an important sense "school" only happens *as* it happens. In this sense, school literally *is* what people do when they identify themselves as "in school."

What makes social life and sociological practice messy and interesting is that both ways of looking at things are true. When I go to one of my classes and sit down with my students, I can feel how the situation of school limits what I see as my options. I know in general what I'm expected to do and what, therefore, would be considered inappropriate for that situation. But as I sit there looking at my students, there's also a sense in the air of "So, what are we going to do?" Even though we all know we're in school and that this means many things are very unlikely to happen, we also don't really know what *is* going to happen because it hasn't happened yet. So, I say something to start things off, or a student asks a question or makes a comment on the reading assignment, or something entirely different happens. And so it goes from there, as "school" unfolds, emerging from how *these* people choose from moment to moment what they're going to *make* of it. If we want to explain what happens during that time, it isn't enough to understand what school is about as a social system, and it isn't enough to understand who the people in the room are as individuals. What happens depends on both/and; it depends both on the situation these people are in and how they choose to participate in it.

What makes things still messier and still more interesting is that in important ways we aren't all in the same situation. Because we occupy a variety of social positions within each system, we tend to experience the situation differently. We are shaped differently by it, limited by it in different ways, and therefore tend to participate differently. So, what school is about will vary depending on whether you're a student or a teacher; female or male; Asian American, Native American, white, Chicano, or African American; older or younger; working class, lower class, middle class, or upper class; immigrant or native; heterosexual, bisexual, lesbian, or gay; employed or unemployed; married or single; a parent or without children. Such characteristics "locate" us in different ways in relation to other people and to systems. They affect how we see ourselves and others, how they see us, and how we treat one another as we participate in making the system happen. When we say that "we are always participating in something larger than ourselves," it's important to remember that "we" is not a homogeneous term. There are multiple "we's" in social life and it's an important part of sociological practice to see how that fact affects what happens.

Into the Practice

All forms of sociological practice are *sociological* because they flow from the same basic questions: What are people participating in, and how are they participating in it? The work can vary in the balance it strikes between the two questions, with some leaning more toward one or the other. A study of how people use language to affect how other people see them, for example, might pay little attention to the social systems where this takes place. Or a study of the world economy might never look at the fine details of how people interact as they participate in it. But the connections between systems and people are always there for us to follow toward a deeper grasp of the complex web that makes up social life. Although the main focus in the rest of this book is on systems, questions about how we figure in all this are never far off, for without people to make systems happen from one moment to the next, there would be no systems to understand nor anyone to care one way or another.

2

Culture: Symbols, Ideas, and the Stuff of Life

As I sit in my office—which also happens to be where I live—and type these words, I hear a loud rumbling sound from what I see as a darkening western sky. In the narrowest sense, when I say "I hear," all that means is that whatever makes the "sound" does it by making the air move. The moving air hits my eardrum and makes it vibrate, and a complex mechanism in the ear turns the vibration into an electrical impulse. The impulse goes to my brain, which then has the experience of "hearing" a sound. And when I "see" a darkening sky, all that happens is that light enters my eye where it's converted to electrical impulses that go to my brain, which turns them into something I experience as a visual image. Of course it doesn't stop there, because almost immediately a string of words flashes across my consciousness: "Uh-oh, thunder." I stop typing. Then more words: "It's gonna rain in the upstairs windows." I go upstairs and close the windows. More words: "I'd better turn off my computer so it doesn't get zapped by lightning." I turn it off, unplug it, and go watch out the window. But no lightning flashes and no rain falls. The western sky gradually clears. "False alarm," I say to myself and go back to writing.

What just happened illustrates a basic aspect of social life that makes it possible. My body had a series of physical experiences—vibrations hit my ears, light entered my eyes, electrical impulses went to my brain. But I didn't leave it at that as I used words to make something of the vibrations and light. I named the rumble "thunder" and the dark sky "rain clouds" and together they became "a thunder and lightning storm on its way." By themselves, the sensations didn't make me do anything; I responded to words and what they meant to me.

When I used words to make what I heard and saw mean something, I constructed a reality on top of the physical sensations. I started thinking about what might happen even though it wasn't happening at the time. "The storm" actually existed only in my imagination and in the words I used to think about it and the damage it might cause. My behavior was based entirely on what I thought. I know this because if I'd thought different words—such as, "the goddess is angry and it's me she's angry at"—I'd have acted quite differently.

We tend to think that we live in the world as it "really" is. In other words, when I hear a rumble and think "thunder," it doesn't occur to me in that moment that I'm doing anything creative. I don't realize that I'm *choosing* a word and using it to attach a particular meaning to the sound. Instead, I act as though the word and the sound are one and the same thing, that the sound is "thunder." In other words, *the reality that really matters to me isn't the sound itself—the moving air that hits my eardrum—but the words and ideas I use to describe it and make it mean something. And that reality is something I carry inside my head.* If I used different words to describe it—"artillery barrage"—I'd create a different reality. By this I don't mean that I create the sound itself when I name it; it is whatever it is. What I do construct is what I think the sound *means* and therefore what it *is* to me, and I use words to do it.

Where do I get the words and where do I get the ideas that go along with them that prompt me to do one thing rather than another? The answer is that I participate in a society that has a *culture,* and that culture contains words and ideas that people can use to name and interpret what they experience. If I lived in a different society with a different culture, then I might have associated that sound with ideas about supernatural beings rather than simply "weather." But I don't, and so I didn't. One of the most remarkable things about human beings is our ability to use culture to create the world we actually live in, to make it up from scratch. Most of what we take for "reality" consists not of things as they "really" are, but of ideas people have developed *about* things as they *think* they are. And culture is where all those ideas wind up, and it's what we look to for the tools we need to make sense of things, including ourselves.

Constructing Reality

Every social system has a culture. My sociology class has one; General Motors has one; Canada has one. Culture consists primarily of symbols—especially the words contained in language—and various kinds of ideas that shape how we think about everything from our relations with other people to the meaning of life. It also includes practices such as music, art, dance, and religious ritual. It includes how we shape the physical world around us, from using sand to make silicon that goes into computer chips to building cities to arranging flowers and plants in that familiar form known as a garden. Culture is both material—the "stuff" of social life—and nonmaterial—the symbols and ideas we use to think and give meaning to just about everything.

Symbols make culture possible, because they're what we use to give something meaning beyond what it otherwise "is." Symbols are building blocks that we use to make sentences, and sentences are what make ideas such as "Thunder means a storm is coming" or "Capitalism is the best economic system in the world." In the simplest sense, when we give something a name—like "thunder"—we create a relationship with it by making it have something to do with us. If we don't have a name for it, we tend not to notice it and not live in relation to it. It doesn't "matter." When we name a dot of light in the sky as a "star," for example, we make it part of a cultural reality. In that sense, we make it real to us in ways that it otherwise wouldn't be, even though that dot of light would still exist up there in the sky. As a species, we miss most of what's around us because there is so much of it and it's impossible to pay attention to more than a tiny portion of it. We use symbols to name things as a way to focus our attention and build a reality to live in. As the philosopher Susanne Langer put it, using symbols to construct reality lies at the heart of what makes us human:

> Only a small part of reality, for a human being, is what is actually going on; the greater part is what he imagines in

connection with the sights and sounds of the moment. . . . It means that his world is bigger than the stimuli which surround him, and the measure of it is the reach of his coherent and steady imagination. An animal's environment consists of the things that act on his senses. . . . He does not live in a world of unbroken space and time, filled with events even when he is not present or when he is not interested; his "world" has a fragmentary, intermittent existence, arising and collapsing with his activities. A human being's world hangs together, its events fit into each other; no matter how devious their connections, there always are connections, in one big framework of time and space. . . . *The world* is something human.[1]

Before going any further, notice the words Langer uses in this passage to refer to people. Every time she uses a pronoun to refer to human beings, it's a masculine "he," "him," or "his." She never uses feminine pronouns or ungendered pronouns such as "they" or "them." Imagine that she'd written the passage in this way:

Only a small part of reality, for human beings, is what is actually going on; the greater part is what they imagine in connection with the sights and sounds of the moment. . . . It means that their world is bigger than the stimuli which surround them, and the measure of it is the reach of their coherent and steady imagination. An animal's environment consists of the things that act on the senses. . . . Animals do not live in a world of unbro-

ken space and time, filled with events even when they
are not present or when they are not interested; their
"world" has a fragmentary, intermittent existence, arising and collapsing with their activities. A human being's
world hangs together, its events fit into each other; no
matter how devious their connections, there always are
connections, in one big framework of time and space. . . .
The world is something human.

In the first version, men are explicitly included by equating
"human" with "male" while women are excluded. Since words
are what we use to construct reality, what is the reality these
words help construct? They construct a world in which men and
what they do are at the center of attention (male-centered), in
which men are used as the standard against which "human" is
measured and judged (male-identified). And they help construct a world in which women are relatively invisible and
thereby devalued and subordinate (male-dominated). It's easy
for me as a man to see myself in the first version, but for a
woman to see herself she has to make a mental leap between
clearly masculine pronouns to "Well, it really means people in
general, which includes me since I'm a person." As a man, I don't
have to go through that to find myself in what we call "humanity," and that's part of my gender privilege as a man in a patriarchal world.

Rather than rush to fault Langer for her use of language, it's
important to note that she wrote this passage in 1962, in a society whose culture offered almost no ideas that would make her
aware of what she was doing. She used language as most people
around her used it and created a reality in her prose that fit com-

fortably with the reality of the culture she lived and wrote in. What she "saw" when she wrote then is different from what I "see" when I read her words now, which is precisely her point and mine.

We can use language to construct all kinds of reality, including what we can't experience through our senses. We can't hear or smell or touch what we call love, for example, like we can a banana. We can see how people treat us, and we might interpret that to mean they love us. But the behavior itself isn't love; it's what we think *means* the person loves us. What we call love is something we think exists beneath what we can see and hear. It's about how people see us and think and feel about us, none of which we can actually observe directly. Someone can say "I love you" or "I feel deeply for you," but the words aren't the love or the feeling; they're *about* the love and the feeling. We use words to construct something we take to be real—the person loves us—and, most important, we act as though what we've created is as real as a chair or a piano. And although—or perhaps because—we can't actually see or hear what the words represent, we may organize a lot of our lives around getting someone to say them to us and prove they really mean what they seem.

Unlike love, an "atom" is something scientists may be able to see someday, but even if they do, for most people it won't exist except as an idea about what the word "atom" supposedly represents. Before the word was invented, what we now think of as atoms simply didn't exist for anyone. Now, however, it's "real" for anyone who's ever taken a high school science class even though we've never actually seen one. All we've seen are words written by people who claim atoms exist, and the words are enough to construct what we then take to be reality. So, there is this thing that I can't see and never will, but a word that names it somehow connects me to it. I can think of my hand, for example, or my computer or eyelashes as something composed of atoms. It's this way with all the words that we use like slender threads connecting us to whatever they point to and name. The words weave a reality, and they connect us to it.

In this sense, the power of symbols goes way beyond labeling things—this is a sugar maple tree, this is love, this is Einstein's theory of relativity. Symbols are also what we use to feel connected to a reality outside of ourselves. Without symbols, a great deal of what we "know" and experience wouldn't exist for us. There would be no memory of what we call the past, except in the form of sensations such as visual imagery or smells; no thinking in the present; and no wondering about what we call the future. Not only would we lose most of our connection to our own past experience, but we'd have no way to share in the experience of others. This is essentially what story-telling traditions are about in many societies and what history is about in others. Back in the 1970s, for example, in my introductory sociology class I used the story of the 1968 Democratic Presidential Convention in Chicago to illustrate how people can perceive the same event in different ways. There was massive antiwar demonstrating outside the convention hall, and the confrontation between demonstrators and police resulted in mayhem and violence. As I watched the events unfold on live television, it seemed to me that the police were rioting and out of control as they attacked nonviolent demonstrators. But when I picked up the next day's edition of a Chicago newspaper, the headlines announced a riot by antiwar demonstrators put down by courageous police officers doing their duty.

In my early years of teaching, I only needed to mention the 1968 Democratic convention for my students to know what I was talking about. But as time passed, there came a day when my new class just sat there without a flicker of recognition. They had no idea what I was talking about, and so I had to tell them a story, string out a river of words that they could then use to connect themselves to something that happened beyond their own experience. I had to construct something that they could then look upon as a chunk of reality, knowing, of course, that a Chicago police officer might have told them a very different kind of story. Later, if someone mentioned the 1968 convention, my students could say, "I know about that," even though they weren't alive when it happened. Now that event is "real" to them, where before it didn't even exist. And mere words made it so.

Beliefs: "I'll See It when I Believe It"

The first purpose of every culture is to provide a way to know what to consider true and what to consider false, and this is what beliefs are about. Notice the difference between "what to *consider* true" and "what *is* true" since what's treated as truth in one culture or historical period may be dismissed as myth or fantasy in another. In Christianity and Judaism, for example, the idea that God exists is obviously true, but for Zen Buddhists, Confucians, and animists the idea of God simply doesn't come up in religious life or anywhere else.

In a sense, symbols are the simplest kind of belief statement, for every dictionary definition declares that something or other is real and exists. If there's a word for something, we're much more likely to "see" it and treat it as real. As recently as a century ago, for example, the word "homosexual" was never used to describe a kind of person, as in "he's a homosexual." It was used instead to describe a kind of sexual behavior without indicating something about a person's social identity. In that sense, homosexuals didn't exist although many people engaged in homosexual behavior of one kind or another. Where before people only saw sexual behavior, now people see "gays," "lesbians," "bi's," and "straights" as distinct types of people. These differences, in turn, are used as a basis for treating people differently, with heterosexuals valued and privileged over everyone else. What people "see" now differs from what people "saw" then because the cultural "truth" of sexual orientation today looks quite different from the "truth" of sexual orientation then. Our dependence on beliefs to determine what's real turns on its head the old expression, "I'll believe it when I see it," or its equivalent, "Seeing is believing." "I'll see it when I believe it" may be closer to the way things really are.

When we string words together to make more complex beliefs, we fashion the world and our place in it. Unlike many Native American cultures, for example, typical European-based cultures see humans and animals as altogether different. The "natural world" and what goes on in it don't include humans. Birds building nests are doing something "natural," but not people building houses. The distinction is completely arbitrary since in each case a species is using its natural abilities to make something that suits it. The fact that we can use our opposable thumbs to manipulate objects like hammers and nails or our brains to invent physics and engineering is no less "natural" than a beaver's ability to chew tree trunks clean through or design a lodge that can withstand a flood.

In Western cultures, however, there is nature on the one hand and humanity on the other. It is a kind of denial that gets us into lots of trouble by setting us up to think of ourselves as separate from the rest of the natural world. It encourages us to live as though we have no deep roots in our environment, the earth, and the cycles of nature. It encourages us to think of ourselves as above the "laws of nature" (since we aren't part of nature), and to suppose that we can get away with things that other species cannot. We act as though we can pollute the environment with chemicals and waste, destroy the ozone level in the atmosphere, exhaust the soil, and cut down the forests and survive and even prosper as other species go extinct all around us. This kind of arrogance makes us dangerous not only to other species, but to ourselves. We may not *believe* we're animals as subject to the "laws" of nature as any bird, but that doesn't mean the kinds of consequences that other animal species cannot escape will leave us untouched. Some years ago, W. I. Thomas and Dorothy Swain Thomas made the classic statement that when cultures define something as real, it has real consequences regardless of whether or not it's actually true. But we also need to consider Robert K. Merton's corollary that what's real has consequences whether we define it as real or not.[2]

Having a set of cultural beliefs allows us to live with a taken-for-granted sense of how things are and to treat the "facts" of our existence as obvious. What we call "obvious," however, isn't necessarily what's true. It's only assumed to be true beyond doubt in a particular culture. Without a sense of the obvious, social life loses its predictability and we lose our basis for feeling secure; but the "obvious" also blinds us to the possibility that what's obviously true might be false. In this sense, when people sometimes accuse sociology of focusing on the obvious, I feel moved to thank them for their recognition and support, because *someone* should be paying attention to what we all go around assuming to be true. What we don't know often gets us into trouble; but even more serious can be what's right under our noses, including what we *think* we know but don't. We feel invested in its being true and defend it, rather than asking if we might have it wrong. United States culture, for example, takes it to be obvious that the country is a political democracy and that capitalist "free enterprise" is democracy's economic equivalent. These beliefs are so powerful that no politician would dare suggest otherwise. It would be political suicide, for example, to suggest there might be something basically wrong with capitalism. No politician could hope to be elected after pointing out that in practice capitalism is anything but democratic since it concentrates economic power in so few hands that enterprise is "free" primarily, if not only, for them.[3] It would be considered disloyal, if not heretical, to question such basic beliefs. But if those beliefs are false or merely hide the truth that underlies the problems that plague us, then the almost sacred protected status of the obvious becomes a trap with us right in the middle.

Values, Choice, and Conflict

In a sense, every cultural idea rests on a belief of some kind because to think about something we first have to see it as something that exists, even if only in our imaginations. But many cultural ideas go beyond basic questions of fact to construct a more complex social reality. Values do this by ranking things in terms of how socially desirable they are—how good or bad, better or worse, superior or inferior they're judged to be.[4] In many cultures, education is valued above ignorance, honesty above dishonesty, profit above loss, kindness above cruelty, cleanliness above filth, married above single, sex above celibacy, rich above poor, heterosexual above gay or lesbian, whiteness above color, male above female, and being in control above not being in control. In each case, cultural beliefs define what's being compared and ranked. We have to know what we mean by "education" or who qualifies as "white" or "heterosexual," and beliefs provide each culture's answer. Values take this a step further with a rough hierarchical order that gives various aspects of social life a vertical dimension. In other words, it's not just that "heterosexual" and "lesbian" differ in what we think they *are*, for cultural values also rank one as preferable to the other.

Values loom large in our lives because they provide a way to choose between alternatives that might otherwise appear equivalent. Almost everything we do involves a choice among different values, although the choice may come so easily to us that we aren't aware of it as such. We decide what clothes to wear each day; whether to work longer hours to earn more money or fewer hours to spend more time doing other things; whether to get a job right after high school or go to college; whether to have sex with someone we feel attracted to; whether to object when we hear sexist, racist, and other forms of oppressive talk; whether to spend the evening watching television or reading; whether to tell friends about our sexual orientation or to keep it to ourselves; whether to vote, and for whom; whether to have an abortion or bear a child; whether to tell friends a truth they'd rather not know. From trivial matters to decisions that can transform our lives, we're always weighing the relative value of what we see as our alternatives, and culture is where we get the ideas we need to do these things.

Values do more than influence how we choose between one course of action and another, for they also affect how we perceive and treat ourselves and other people. When values rank European above Latina, for example, or male above female, or physically able above disabled, people are sorted into different places in a social hierarchy of worth. This makes problems like social oppression more than seeing differences among people, but of ranking entire categories of people in ways that exclude and devalue some and include and privilege others. It can be as monumental as the Bosnian-Serb genocidal war of "ethnic cleansing" or as subtle as a white waiter seating a black customer next to the kitchen door and never coming back to take an order; but in every case, what's at stake is the dignity and worth of human beings.

Like every other aspect of culture, values have a taken-for-granted quality about them. We experience them as a natural part of reality, not as socially constructed ideas *about* reality. Our preference for what we value feels so immediate and comes so easily that we assume it's just part of the human experience, that there wasn't a time or a place when people didn't feel this way. For some preferences, this is probably true. Even infants would rather be warm than cold, comfortable than in pain, full rather than hungry. But most of what we value is what we learn to value through socialization in a particular culture. A powerful way to see this is to experience cultures that promote different values. A few years ago, for example, I traveled to Norway to visit relatives. We spent several days in the city of Oslo, where the exten-

sive train system runs within the city and outward toward surrounding communities. I was startled to notice trains without
conductors to collect fares or punch tickets, and train and subway stations with no way to make sure people paid their fares—
no gates, no turnstiles, no ticket booths. I watched people board
the train, take out a multiple-ride ticket and insert it in a machine that punched it each time they rode the train; and I saw
people buy single-ride tickets from machines on station platforms and then put the tickets in their pockets since there was
no one to collect them.

I can't imagine buses and trains in the United States operating in this way, and the reason is that the two societies have such
different cultures. Norwegian culture includes beliefs that the
train system essentially belongs to everyone, that it can't keep
running if people don't pay their fares, and that most people will
therefore pay as part of doing their share. The culture also places
a higher value on trust than it does on making sure no one gets
away without paying. It also places a higher value on a sense of
belonging to the community and doing your bit to make it work
than it does on getting something for nothing. In the United
States, however, the belief is that most people won't pay if they
can get it for nothing, and that getting something for nothing is
more important than a sense of community and shared purpose.
There are exceptions, especially in smaller communities. In the
little town where I live, for example, it's common in the summer
to see roadside stands with fruits and vegetables for sale and no
one there to collect money, just an open "cash" box and a sign
that posts prices. And some colleges—including the one where I
teach—have student honor codes instead of exam proctors and
other kinds of "policing" to prevent student cheating. In both

cases a value choice is being made in how to organize the system. I'm sure some people take vegetables without paying and some students cheat and get away with it, and this goes against some important values. But something regarded as even more valuable is gained, for people are able to live and work in an atmosphere of mutual trust and respect that's hard to maintain if we're always assuming that everyone will cheat whenever they get the chance.

The more I see of other cultures, the more aware I am of my own culture *as* a culture, and that things aren't just what they *are* but are what my culture makes them out to be. I can also see that when I make choices, I always choose from a limited range of alternatives offered by my culture. This suggests that we never make anything like a "free" choice. As the philosopher Arthur Schopenhauer put it, when it comes to values "We want what we will, but we don't will what we want."[5] In other words, when I feel myself wanting a new car, I don't realize how my wanting it is connected to a cultural value placed on material possessions—more stuff is better than less; new stuff is better than old; stuff I don't have is better than stuff I do. Since we're socialized into a set of cultural values and don't choose how that happens, the values we acquire limit us in ways that are hard to see until we step outside and realize they aren't the only possibilities. In that sense, my "freedom" to want a car is limited by a culture that sets me up to value having a car more than, say, being spiritually enlightened or helping people less well-off than I am. It also sets me up to see the accumulation of material wealth as an essential part of a happy and successful life. This is true of just about everything we value. Whether it's using plastic surgery to "improve" how we look, aspiring to a college education, laughing at sexist jokes as a way to "fit in," or seeing our country as superior to all others, we rarely realize how much our culture limits our preferences to a narrow range of possibilities. And we also don't realize how radically different our options might be somewhere else.

As an individual, I can be aware that culture exists and shapes my perceptions and experience, including what I think I want. As someone born and raised in the United States, I can see how materialistic my culture is and choose to live my life differently by pursuing other values. But I'll always be doing this *in spite* of my cultural background, as an act of going against what I was raised to value as a path of least resistance. I can expand my "freedom" only by liberating myself from the narrow range of choices that my culture—that any culture—offers the people who participate in it. To do this, I need to "step outside" the cultural framework I'm used to so that I can see it *as* a framework, as one possibility among many. Stepping outside is an important part of what sociological practice is about, and concepts like "culture," "beliefs," and "values" are important tools used in the process for they point to what we're stepping outside *of*.

We can go against our culture because cultures aren't rigid frameworks that determine who we are and what we do. Values can't tell us what to do in every possible situation, because most situations involve combinations of values that are impossible to predict. Instead of giving us clear rules for how to choose in every situation, values provide general guidelines for how to weigh one alternative against another. As social psychologist Roger Brown put it, values are like rules of grammar that we use to interpret sentences that we've never seen before.[6] How we apply those rules, however, is up to us. It's generally regarded as "good," for example, to choose honesty over dishonesty. But what happens when that value conflicts with another such as love of family? If murderers looking for my brother ask me where he is, you can be sure that I'll do what I can to send them off in the wrong direction. But what if it's my brother who's the murderer? What if I'm in the position of David Kaczynski who realized his brother Theodore might be the "Unabomber" whose package bombs killed several people and severely injured numerous others? Do I turn him in for almost certain imprisonment or death, or do I choose loyalty to kin as a higher value and remain silent? There is no book of answers to such questions, which is what makes value conflict an enduring source of struggle and anguish. It comes up over and over again, whether about protecting the environment at the expense of jobs or making birth control and sex education available in schools. Values provide us with raw materials and rough guidelines for weighing alternatives, but they can't tell us how to use them.

As part of any culture, values map out paths of least resistance that shape how people participate in systems. As a way to regulate people's behavior, however, they can only suggest how we *ought* to behave. What they lack is something to back them up and turn them into statements about how we *must* behave *or else*. Adding the "or else" to a value gives us something stronger—a norm.

Norms, Morality, and Deviance

The difference between what is valued and desired and what is expected and required is social consequences in the form of rewards and punishments. If you take a cultural value and turn it into a rule enforced with rewards and punishments, then you have a norm, a value "with teeth" that can bite if you don't choose it. When David Kaczynski decided whether or not to turn in his brother, he had more to do than weigh competing values. He also had to consider his behavior in relation to norms and the punishments and rewards that go with them. On the one hand, if he turned his brother in, he'd be rewarded by a grateful public for ending a nightmare of violence against innocent people. At the same time, he may have been punished by family members for violating family norms based on loyalty to kin. On the other hand, if he remained silent, he risked being shamed by a public outraged at his disregard for future victims of his brother's violence. His family, however, might have rewarded him for his loyalty to kin. In either case, his dilemma wasn't simply choosing between "better" or "worse" alternatives. There were real social consequences that hinged on what he chose to do.

Notice how changing the system he participates in can change the social consequences of his actions. If his family was formed around both kinship *and* organized crime activities, then his situation might look quite different. Instead of choosing between his duty to society and loyalty to his brother, he'd also have to consider what would happen if turning in his brother caused the police to take a close look at his family. To avoid that, he might turn his brother in, not to the police, but to his family who might then deal with the brother in its own way to protect the family's "business" interests.

Like every aspect of culture, norms are made up. They aren't what people do; they are ideas *about* what people do. Like beliefs, they refer to some aspect of reality, such as the definition of "murder." Like values, norms are linked to cultural judgments about what's considered more or less desirable: Murder is bad; killing to protect your country is good. Norms go a step further, however, by linking beliefs and values to social consequences that wouldn't otherwise happen. If a man sets off a bomb near a crowd of people, the result might be injury or death. Whether he'd be arrested and what would happen to him then, however, depends on what the norms look like, and these can be changed any time a law-making body decides. If he's punished, it won't be simply because he hurt or killed people; it'll be because he violated a norm that prohibits such killing. To see the difference, consider how he might have used a bomb to kill people with different consequences. If he flew a bomber during wartime, for example, he'd be rewarded for accomplishing his mission, especially if he was courageous in doing so. The *objective* consequences might be the same—a bomb explodes and kills people—but the *social* consequences depend on the norms that apply in *that* system. If his plane were shot down after he dropped his bombs, he might be prosecuted as a criminal by his captors if *their* norms defined the killing as an act of murder. In short, we can't tell what the social consequences of an action will be unless we know about the culture of the social system we're operating in.

Norms are ideas not only about how people behave, but about how they appear and, in some cases, who they are. If you walk naked down Main Street at noon on a cold January day, the objective consequence might be that you'd catch a cold or people would see what your body looks like. The social consequences, however, would most likely be something more—from disapproving looks to being arrested. In a nudist colony, however, the consequence would be social acceptance and disapproving looks would be reserved for people who went around with*out* taking off their clothes. Norms about personal appearance can be so powerful that we feel bound by them even when we're by ourselves. I was once camping by a lake in a remote section of Vermont, for example, when I decided to go for a swim. I was standing in a beautiful grove of birch trees with no one but my wife for miles around, taking off my clothes and about to put on a bathing suit. Suddenly, with one foot in and one foot out, I was stopped by a question that popped into my head: Why am I putting this suit on? Unable to think of a good reason, I took a wonderful (and rare) skinny dip, beyond the reach of my culture's norms.

At such moments, I wonder why norms exist in the first place. Why should anyone care if we wear clothes or not, or clothes that are "appropriate" for the occasion? Why should such rules matter so much that people might be ridiculed or shunned or even arrested and locked up for breaking them? For that matter, why should we feel justified in shooting someone who's running off with a television we consider to be our "property"? The answer lies through deeper questions of what societies are all about, which, like most important questions, have more than one answer.

One answer comes from what's known as the functional perspective, which is based on the idea that every social system has certain requirements that must be met for it to work. From this perspective, norms exist because without them systems would fall apart or foul up in one way or another. This makes sense given that social systems are organized around relationships among people, and relationships consist largely of what we expect of one another. Since norms define and enforce expectations, it follows that a social system can't do without them.

Norms also play an important part in defining a system's boundaries by giving us a way to tell insiders from outsiders and by controlling who gets to be one or the other. To belong to a community, for example, you have to go along with its culture to a certain degree, and you can often tell members from non-members by who does and who doesn't. If you break the rules, you risk punishment, including being thrown out altogether. This isn't simply because you've violated a norm, but because the norms are connected to beliefs and values that define reality and what's considered important. The surest way to gain acceptance and influence in a group is to adopt its culture openly and from the outset. Rejecting a culture is the surest way to be rejected yourself no matter what else you might have to contribute. So, when new students flood our campus in the fall, they wander around looking lost much of the time, because they *are* lost, and this makes it easy to pick them out from a crowd. They break rules left and right because they don't know the rules are even there, and we forgive them for awhile. But there comes a point when we expect them to know what's what and hold them accountable for what they do as the price of being included. They've crossed a boundary defined in part by their relationship to a set of cultural ideas about who they are in relation to something larger than themselves.

In this sense, it doesn't matter what the norms actually are in a system so long as there are some. When children create a club, for example, one of the first things they do is make up rules that have to be obeyed in order to belong. To have a club without rules is unthinkable, no matter how silly or contradictory they might be. The rules themselves don't matter; what matters is establishing a sense of something larger that members can feel part of, which, in turn, also tells them something about who they are. The great French sociologist Émile Durkheim saw this collective sense of "we" as the necessary foundation of social life and the only way to control people's behavior.[7] It's what morality is really all about—not just a set of rules about how to be a good person, but a shared sense of what the essence of a social system and its people consists of. It's from that shared sense of "us" and "it" that morality draws much of its power and authority, for to violate moral rules is to risk our sense of belonging to the system itself. The most important thing about morality isn't behavior, but the feeling of attachment that binds people to a group or society when they support its moral rules. Without this, people feel lost and systems fall apart.

From this perspective, when someone breaks a rule they do much more than that, for they also violate a sense of boundaries and raise questions about who they are in relation to an entire system and its culture. If you wear the "wrong" clothes to work, people start wondering if you really belong there, if you're really committed to what the place is "all about." You might think, "What's a dress code got to do with morality?" In the usual sense of what makes a good person, the answer is probably "not much" in most systems most of the time. But in a larger sociological sense, morality is a basis for defining what a group or society is all about and what it takes to be accepted as a member. This makes the answer more complex. Whether it's rules about killing people or how to behave at the dinner table, *all* norms have some bearing on belonging and commitment that can tell us as much about what we're about as they do about the systems we participate in.

If morality is basically about belonging, then it follows that people who are seen as outsiders will be treated as deviants, as violators of a moral code. This is what happens with stigma, when people are treated as deviant not because of something they've done, but because of who they are.[8] This often plays a key role in various forms of social inequality and oppression. In many ways, characteristics such as race, gender, ethnicity, sexual orientation, physical ability, and religion are often used to define deviant categories of people who are then treated as outsiders by dominant groups. They are denied the normal, everyday benefits of belonging, from being treated with courtesy and respect in a store to being able to find a place to live, a decent school for their children, or a job that reflects their abilities. For centuries, for example, women have been regarded as deviants—as incomplete, flawed versions of men, whose minds and bodies render them weak and not up to the standard of a fully-developed and competent human being.[9] In most valued occupations and professions, women are still treated as outsiders and are told in ways both subtle and overt that they have no right to be there and are unwelcome. Whether it's not being invited to join a group of men going out for a beer after work or finding a used condom in her desk drawer and other forms of sexual harassment, the underlying message and its effect are the same.[10]

The use of norms to exclude and oppress entire categories of people suggests something going on that a functionalist perspective doesn't see. It makes sense that systems need to regulate what people *do*, but it makes much less sense to argue that systems have to regulate who people *are* in terms of something like the color of their skin. It is hard to see why a society would require arrangements that not only elevate and privilege some groups, but that routinely inflict suffering on everyone else.

Systematic patterns of exclusion, exploitation, domination, and abuse make more sense from what's known in sociological practice as the conflict perspective. The conflict perspective also focuses on systems but primarily as a setting for conflict between groups that result in patterns of inequality. Culture is where we get most of the ideas we use to define reality, to differentiate "superior" from "inferior," and to identify the "rules" of the game. It is therefore not surprising that privileged groups use their power and influence to shape culture itself in their own interests, including the protection of their privilege.

Consider, for example, cultural ideas about "private property." The idea of private property hasn't been around very long, dating back no more than several thousand years. For something to be regarded as property, it has to occupy a particular position in a social relationship. When I say that the land my house sits on is my property, I'm saying that the people of my community and society recognize my right to live on it and do pretty much what I want with it, although not without limits. This allows me to control who comes onto the property and how they treat it. With few exceptions, my property can't be changed or destroyed or taken away from me without my consent, unless it's done by a nonhuman force such as an earthquake. In this sense, property isn't something (or, in the case of slaves, some*one*). Instead, property is a set of *ideas* about the relationships that connect "owners," what's *regarded* as their property, and other people and social systems such as communities and societies.

What we call "property" exists only when cultures have beliefs that define it as real. Like many North American tribes, for example, the Wampanoag traditionally viewed land as part of nature and not something that people could own. They could live on it, farm it, hunt on it, worship it, and admire its beauty, but they couldn't treat is as "property." When English settlers came to the island of Nantucket off the southern coast of Massachusetts, however, they "purchased" land from the Wampanoag tribe. The Wampanoag were dumbfounded by what the settlers did next: They arrested and punished anyone who "trespassed" on "their property." The Wampanoag could no longer walk on or otherwise use the land because it no longer "belonged" to them. Wampanoag culture had no place for such ideas, and eventually died out without ever acquiring one. To them, the norms of English culture defined a relationship to the land that simply wasn't possible.

In theory, norms that protect private property serve the interests of everyone who has any, whether it's my VCR or Exxon's oil wells. And the more property you own, the more you'll benefit from that protection. But protection takes on much greater significance when property is a basis for systems of social inequality. When owning property gives people power and privilege over others, then any norm that protects property rights also protects the inequality of power and privilege and what people are able to do with it. In the United States, for example, as in most industrial capitalist societies, a tiny portion of the population owns or controls the vast majority of wealth, especially the factories, machinery, tools, and other resources that people use to produce wealth and to make a living. The wealthiest 20 percent of U.S. families owns 80 percent of all the wealth; the top 10 percent owns 70 percent; and the wealthiest 1 percent owns almost 40 percent. By comparison, the bottom 40 percent owns barely 2 percent. Across the world as a whole, the pattern is much the same, with the top 20 percent owning 85 percent of all wealth and the bottom 40 percent owning 2 percent.[11]

A lopsided distribution of wealth doesn't mean that norms that protect private property exist only for the elite who own most of it. It does mean, however, that while the law protects everyone's property, it also enables the elite to maintain its privileged position, including its ability to increase its share of wealth even further. If you own or control businesses and factories, you can decide who works and who doesn't, how they work, and what becomes of the goods and services they produce. You can decide whether to close up shop and move production and jobs to another region or country where labor costs are lower and profit margins are therefore higher. You can tell communities and states that unless they give your company tax breaks, you'll move to "a friendlier business climate." And when states and communities agree rather than see the jobs go elsewhere, the people who live and work there have to make up the lost taxes or make do with less money for schools and other government services.

Seeing how different aspects of social life fit together is an important part of sociological practice, for everything in social life is connected to something else. Notice, for example, that a culture can't include values and norms about property unless it also has a cultural belief that defines such a thing as property as real in the first place. Notice also that norms that seem to support one value are likely to affect other values as well, so that what appears to be just about protecting property can also be about preserving an entire social order based on privilege and inequality. This is true of every aspect of social life: The connections that we see right away and most easily are usually just the tip of the iceberg. In this way, sociological practice can take us beneath the surface toward the deeper truth of what's going on, why it matters, and what it's got to do with us.

Attitudes: Culture as Feeling

Beliefs, values, and norms have a huge influence on how we perceive reality, how we think about it, and how we behave. If we look at heterosexist prejudice, for example, we can see how elements of all three kinds of ideas combine. Prejudice against gays and lesbians values one sexual orientation as superior to others. The values are typically propped up by beliefs that define sexual orientation as a type of person and make heterosexuals look better. Heterosexuality, for example, may be seen as "natural" and healthy while homosexuality is seen as "unnatural," a disease or perversion; stereotypes portray homosexuals as more likely than heterosexuals to exploit children sexually, even though the truth is just the opposite. Since heterosexist prejudice elevates one sexual orientation above others, it becomes a form of privilege, in that heterosexuals are treated better than gays and lesbians simply because of their sexual orientation. Like all privilege, heterosexual privilege is supported and maintained by norms that in various ways keep gays and lesbians "in their place" by discriminating against them in areas such as housing, work, and parental and spousal rights. A lesbian couple might live together and share their lives for twenty years, and yet if one becomes seriously ill, her parents and not her life partner are likely to be the ones legally recognized as having the right to manage her care if she can't do it for herself.

As powerful as beliefs, values, and norms are, they don't account for the feelings involved, the emotional component of prejudice. Hatred, disgust, or fear directed at gays and lesbians isn't a belief or a value or a norm, even though it may be closely connected to them. Straight men may feel contempt for gay men, for example, and connect it to beliefs and values that render gays contemptible in straight men's eyes. And they may act out their contempt through norms that disadvantage and oppress gays. But none of these are the feeling of contempt itself. The feeling is a cultural attitude that blends belief, value, and emotion in ways that shape how we feel and behave toward people or, for that matter, the earth, ideas, or just about anything else.[12] The feelings can be as intense and momentous as unbridled public hatred. Or they can be subtle and everyday, in the hidden sense of unease straight men often feel when they're around gay men.[13] In each case, the feeling is more than an emotion, for it's an emotion rooted in a social situation and a culture that goes with it. Feelings depend on how people define the reality of what's going on, what matters most, and what's expected of them and regarded as socially appropriate. Whether the most intense heterosexist hatred in a hate crime or the most restrained formal politeness at the dinner table, attitudes are a complex blend of ideas and feelings that shape how people participate in social life.

Some emotions are probably hard-wired into us as a species. Small children, for example, don't have to be taught to feel afraid. Fear is certainly an emotion, but it's not a cultural attitude unless it's connected to beliefs or values. Some years ago, for example, our household added a snake to our two dogs and two goats. When I first heard the suggestion, I reacted as most people in this society would: "Why would you want to do *that?*" I asked. I was persuaded to consider that there was no reason to feel afraid or disgusted other than what I'd learned from cultural attitudes about snakes. I went, I saw, I touched, and discovered much to my surprise that this creature was in fact a gentle being with skin that felt like fine leather. Perhaps most important, I realized that for all my bad feelings about snakes, this animal had far more to fear from me than I from it. It can barely hear or see and explores it's environment primarily by smelling with its tongue. I could kill it whenever I wanted, and it would barely see death coming. It, however, would never strike at me unless it felt threatened, and, even then, couldn't hurt me very much unless it got lucky. When I tell this story to people, they almost always react with a mixture of disgust and fear, even though only a few of them have been close enough to a snake to hold it or look in its face. Their fear isn't about actual experience. It's about growing up and living in a culture that's full of evil and frightening images of snakes.

In one sense, then, attitudes can be primary emotions like fear that are attached to various cultural beliefs and values. By itself, fear isn't an attitude, but a cultural fear of snakes is. Many attitudes, however, are emotions that exist *only* in relation to a social context. Contempt and disgust, for example, only exist as expressions of negative judgments, and you can't judge something without using beliefs and values. You can teach infants to fear just about anything—a banana, a person—just by pairing it with something inherently fearful such as violence. But you can't teach infants to feel disgust for something, because they have no way to form ideas and judgments about anything until they learn to use language. Put something delicious in an infant's mouth, and it'll be gone in no time. But put the same thing in my mouth *and* tell me that it's ground dog (a delicacy in many parts of Asia) and it won't stay in my mouth for long. My reaction of disgust wouldn't be because of the taste, but because of the ideas I'd use to think about what I was eating. Give someone a delicious hamburger and, when they're half through eating it, tell them it's ground cat and watch how they react and you'll see the power of cultural attitudes in action. Even if you then tell them it's not cat, they may still refuse to eat it.

The mix of emotion, beliefs, and values is at the core of what makes a cultural attitude. Pride, shame, guilt, love, hate, loyalty, reverence, respect, disrespect, haughtiness, humility, pity, patriotism, sympathy, empathy, gratitude, arrogance—all exist only in relation to ideas about the object of the feeling. This is also true of what's often thought to be an absence of emotion, as in attitudes of detachment or emotional deadness. In this sense, there's no such thing as being "unemotional": "Unfeeling" is as much an emotional state as "deeply moved" or "enraged." Very often, when people say they don't feel anything, they're feeling a kind of flat emptiness that's very much a feeling even though they may not call it that. And it's a feeling that can shape how they behave in powerful ways. It can mask and underlie great cruelty, for example, or make it easier for people to kill thousands in warfare, to do things that might sicken and horrify them if they allowed themselves to feel *those* feelings instead of the feeling of flat, detached "I'm-just-doing-my-job" efficiency that often takes their place.

Although we don't think of it as such in this culture, "unemotional" is a powerful attitude that is especially expected of men and, not surprisingly, those in positions of power. The only emotion that's routinely allowed and encouraged in men is anger, because it, like being emotionally detached, makes it easier to exercise power and control. Since many cultures link standards for true manhood and leadership to men's ability to keep themselves in a seemingly unemotional state, anyone who aspires to those positions will feel drawn toward that attitude. The attitude combines a feeling of emotional detachment with cultural beliefs about the consequences of allowing various kinds of emotions to influence judgments and decisions. It's also connected to values that rank stereotypical masculine inexpressiveness above the stereotypical feminine tendency to be openly "emotional." So, women, who are culturally encouraged as women to be "emotional," will tend toward an "unemotional" attitude if they want to be taken seriously and succeed in the male-dominated business and professional world. This happens with many forms of social inequality in that those in lower positions are often culturally stereotyped as more emotional than those in higher positions and this can easily be used against them. When blacks or women express anger at discrimination in the workplace, for example, they risk triggering stereotypes of blacks and women as overly emotional and therefore out of control and needing to be controlled by others. This, in turn, is used to argue that they're unsuited for higher positions because they don't display appropriate attitudes.

Looking at attitudes and how they work is a useful way for seeing how various aspects of culture combine to produce complex and powerful results. Although culture consists primarily of what we can't see—symbols, ideas, and feelings—it also includes what we can, the material world that humans construct as part of their social environment.

Material Culture and the Stuff of Life

The reality we construct is both nonmaterial and material. As a form of culture, for example, we can think of music as patterns of sound that we recognize as music rather than noise. In many cultures, music is expressed in a symbolic form using notes, sharps, flats, rests, and the like, which musicians must know in order to "read" what other musicians write (although they can play music without being able to read it). But as a part of culture, music also has a material basis for its existence, from the paper it's printed on to the brass, wood, steel, animal skins, shells, and other materials that go into making instruments. In industrial societies, the hardware for producing and reproducing music seems to expand daily, from microphones, mixers, and tape recorders to electric violins, synthesizers, and computer software that may someday be able to take music as it's played and print it out on paper. What all of this means for sociological practice is that to understand music or any other part of social life, we have to pay attention to both its material and nonmaterial aspects and how they're related to one another. The terms of social life aren't simply embodied in who we are as people; they're also embodied in how we shape the physical world, from the furniture we sit on to the cities and towns we live and work in.

Material culture exists because human beings seem to have an inherent tendency to transform the world as we find it. Whether it's to cut a path through the woods from the village to the water hole, or to plant a garden, lay down a highway, build a house, or turn iron ore into steel, we seem bent toward the creative work of turning one thing into something else. How we do this matters on several levels. In the most immediate sense, the material world we create directly affects our own physical existence. The telephone, for example, takes our limited ability to hear and extends it across thousands of miles. In the opposite direction, the walls of buildings—especially windowless ones in buildings where many people work—can shut us in and close us off from the world around us and the people in it. By itself, the human body isn't able to do very much. Our senses of smell, sight, hearing, taste, and touch don't measure up very well with those of many species. We can't fly, and most mammals can outrun or outswim us without too much trouble. In the overall scheme of things, in short, we're an awkward and limited bunch. But our ability to invent material culture more than makes up for it, which is both a blessing and a curse. The blessing is that we can do creative things that otherwise would be far beyond our reach. The curse is that we can use material culture to do damage beyond our wildest imaginations. The human ability to pollute and otherwise destroy the life-sustaining capacity of the planet is so vast and complex that we're only beginning to grasp the scope of it. And our ability to use technology not only to eradicate entire species whose presence we find objectionable, but to slaughter other human beings in huge numbers continues to increase with no apparent end in sight.

Beyond our physical existence, material culture also affects the terms on which social life is lived. It affects how we perceive reality, how we feel, what we value and expect from other people, and how social relationships are structured around things like the distribution of power. When Johannes Gutenberg invented movable type in the fifteenth century, for example, he helped bring about a social revolution. For the first time, it was possible to take information or an idea, reproduce it in written form, and distribute it to a huge audience. This meant that it now mattered whether most people could read and write, because when books were printed by hand, only the wealthy could afford them. As literacy spread, ideas, information, innovation, and invention spread right along with it.

In the simplest sense, a printing press is just machine, a collection of parts arranged in a certain way. Its social significance comes from how it's used, especially in choosing what to print. Since what people read influences how they perceive and think about the world, it was inevitable that groups would struggle over control of the printing press as a way to control the flow of information and ideas in societies. At one time or another just about every government in the world has tried to limit people's access to printing presses and what they print on them. In the early 1980s, the Romanian government went so far as to require people who owned typewriters to register them with the police so that the authorities could use samples of their type to identify the origin of antigovernment writing. If you had a criminal record or were seen as someone who posed "a danger to public order and security," you couldn't own a typewriter at all.[14]

In less authoritarian societies, the state has less control over printing and publishing. This doesn't mean that most people have access to this material culture, however, because it's quite expensive. As a result, writes Michael Parenti, freedom of the press exists primarily for those who own the presses or have the money to buy space in newspapers and magazines and print what they want to say.[15] Increasingly, the public flow of ideas and information is controlled by a shrinking number of corporations that expand by merging and buying one another. This is happening across the mass media, from television, radio, and film to books, magazines, and newspapers. The rate of acquisitions, mergers, and the consolidation of power and control is so rapid that it's difficult to keep up with who owns whom. It's hard to find a major book publisher, for example, that isn't owned by someone else, usually a still larger publisher, but increasingly a corporation that otherwise has nothing to do with publishing.

Why does this matter? It matters because what can appear to be a diversity of independent news, information, and analysis can in fact flow from a small number of sources whose interests take first priority. As one commentator put it in response to a series of acquisitions and mergers (which have since undoubtedly been superseded by still more shuffling of ownership, power, and control):

> Watch a Little, Brown book become a Book of the Month Club pick, a Warner paperback and a Warner Brothers film that is featured in *People*, reviewed in *Time*, with a soundtrack album on Atlantic Records, shown on *HBO*, parodied in *Mad* and finally developed into a TV series by Lorimar. And all of the money— along with all of the choices—will be left in the hands of Time Warner, Inc.[16]

What looks like a free and open "marketplace of ideas" turns out to be something else altogether.

Social control over the flow of ideas would be an issue even without the trend toward consolidating power in mass media. Almost none of the media, for example, have anything serious to say about capitalism and how it affects most people's lives. If you want to learn more about this, you won't find it on television or radio, even on the supposedly liberal-biased public networks. Nor will you find it in newspapers, news magazines, or the lists of major book publishers. Why not? It could be that there simply isn't anything critical to say because capitalism is so close to perfection that, aside from minor flaws, it is about as good as an economy can get. Given the amount of suffering and crisis that has become almost routine in the world, however, it's unlikely that we've arrived at such an exalted final state. It's more likely that the mass media are silent on the subject of capitalism because they are organized in ways that make silence a path of least resistance. For example, almost all of the mass media are capitalist corporations. As such, most are owned by stockholders looking for the highest return on their investment and controlled by executives whose fortunes depend on how well they serve stockholders' interests. In other words, those who own and control the mass media have a vested interest in preserving and promoting capitalism as an economic system. They have little to gain and a considerable amount to lose by suggesting there might be something wrong with it. This makes them unlikely to question or undermine what makes their power and privilege possible.

None of this means the mass media control *what* we think about a particular issue; but they do have a great deal of control over what we think *about*. And if they can control *whether* we see something like capitalism as an issue, they don't have to worry about *how* we see it as an issue. In this sense, the most profound use of media power isn't in what's printed, filmed, or broadcast; it's in what's not. It's no wonder that even as major social problems like social inequality and chronic economic insecurity affect more and more people, it doesn't occur to them to ask how a system as powerful and pervasive as capitalism might be part of the problem.

Clearly the problem has less to do with the existence of material culture, like the printing press or television camera, than it does with how it's used in a particular system. If we overlook the difference between the thing and how it's used, it's easy for material culture to take on a life of its own, as if it has power over us all by itself. Computers, for example, take a lot of blame for supposedly controlling people's lives. But the problem isn't the machine; it's in our relationship to it and how we think about it, both of which we can control more than we know. A computer is, after all, just metal and plastic and amounts to nothing more than that unless someone plugs it in, turns it on, and tells it what to do. As such, it's nothing more than what we make it to be, and has no more significance than we choose to give it. In the early stages of the Industrial Revolution in Europe, workers saw machines as evil because machines were being used to replace and control workers. The words "saboteur" and "sabotage," in fact, are based on the practice of taking wooden-soled shoes—*sabots*—and throwing them in the "works" to disable or ruin the hated machines.

As the twentieth century ends, the use of machines to replace and control workers is expanding rapidly, primarily in the form of computers and robots. There's nothing about the machinery itself, however, that requires anyone to use it this way. More efficient production could be used to reduce the number of hours people work and still provide enough goods and services to meet everyone's needs. In a capitalist economic system, however, this isn't what "efficient" means. A capitalist organization increases efficiency by maximizing production and minimizing cost—especially the cost of labor—which leads to higher profits. So, the "leisure" that workers gain from the increased use of "labor saving" technology tends to be the spare time afforded by unemployment, rather than a full-time job that demands less from them in return for "a living." Amidst a technological explosion, people in the United States aren't working less, they're working more and without a great deal to show for it.[17]

The stuff of material culture can't tell us what it's about. For that we have to see where material culture fits in a social system, how people perceive, value, and think about it, and what they do with it. As such, material culture can take social life in many different directions at once. The computer, for example, can be used as an instrument of oppressive control. It can store enormous amounts of personal information about people and be used to invade their privacy and monitor their every movement in the workplace. In some businesses, workers must use a coded key card to enter or leave any room, including the bathroom. This provides information about where workers are from one moment to the next throughout the day, even at times when you might think it is no one's business but their own.

Technology, however, can serve any purpose we can imagine. The Internet and World Wide Web computer networks, for example, allow anyone with a computer, a modem, and a phone line to connect to an entire worldwide communications system that—so far—is virtually impossible for anyone to control. The Internet and the Web consist of millions of individual computers connected in small networks that are themselves connected to one another to make larger networks. No one knows from one day to the next how many computers are involved; and certainly no one can know all of the billions of possible routes that connect those computers to one another. There are no central switching stations as there are in telephone systems, no centralized control points to shut down or regulate the flow of information. If one computer network isn't working, then information is simply routed to its destination through one of countless other networks. Messages don't even travel in single units: A message sent over the Internet is broken down into "packets," which are then sent off in different directions and reassembled in their original form at their destination. It's virtually impossible to control such a decentralized system as a whole, which is why governments interested in controlling the flow of information—which includes most governments—are working hard to invent technology to control cyberspace.

Although material culture gets relatively little attention in sociological work, it can play a complex and paradoxical role in social life. We create it and make it part of our identities, and yet we often experience it as separate and external—autonomous and powerful in relation to ourselves. We identify with it in the sense that we come to depend on it so heavily that we can't imagine life without it. At the same time, we forget that it's nothing more than something people have made. The danger of identifying with material culture is that we may hang onto it even when it produces terrible consequences. We think we can't live without cars, air conditioning, and nuclear power plants; but the long-term truth may be that we can't live with them. There is also danger in seeing material culture as alien and separate from our ability to create it. It's dangerous because even if we want to change it or get rid of it, we feel helpless or, worse, that it's not our responsibility in the first place. This is how we can find ourselves feeling and acting as if we're at the mercy of inanimate objects.

It's all too easy to forget that the sum total of any culture is the product of the abundant potential of human imagination. "We live in a web of ideas, a fabric of our own making," wrote philosopher Susanne Langer.[18] But as we live inside this web, what it appears to be at the moment is always only a piece of what's possible. This profoundly limits our ability to grasp the larger sense of what's going on. We live as though inside a little box of reality constructed from cultural stuff—whether in a family, at work, or in society at large. And we rarely see beyond it, primarily because we don't even know the box is there. We act as though what we see is simply all there is. But it's not, and to imagine something more, we first have to see *it* for what it is. In other words, to see *beyond* the box, we first have to take a serious look *at* the box, and that's what sociological practice is about.

Our Box: The Best Box, the Only Box

Living inside a box we can't see out of makes it easy to assume that every culture must be just like ours, a phenomenon known as ethnocentrism. We're like infants who see themselves and their experience as the center of the universe. The box goes with us wherever we go, including to other societies, which, of course, have cultures of their own. I vividly remember being deep inside Mexico some years ago and hearing a U.S. tourist's angry outburst at a restaurant waiter who wouldn't accept dollars as payment for the meal. The tourist couldn't imagine a place where dollars weren't the currency of choice and refused to allow any other possibility. His tone conveyed the unmistakable message that being from the United States gave him a sense of arrogant entitlement in relation to a Third World country: "Who are you to refuse my money?" But it also reflected an underlying phenomenon that is nearly universal—the difficulty in seeing beyond our own culture.

The tourist's blindness to cultural difference was ethnocentric, but he was also ethnocentric in his assumption that any culture other than his own was inferior. He assumed that U.S. dollars were a superior currency to Mexican pesos, and that the waiter should accept if not be grateful for an offering of this exalted currency. In fact, however, at that time the peso had a much more stable history of maintaining its value than did the dollar and, if anything, it was the U.S. tourist who held an "inferior" currency. But in a world seen through ethnocentric eyes, none of that mattered. The tourist resisted anything that might raise questions about the comfortable box he lived in, beginning with awareness of the box itself and the possibility of alternatives to it.

Ethnocentrism is everywhere and not peculiar to any culture. It is what led Europeans to call the Americas "the New World" and to assume the right to name it and conquer its peoples and plunder its resources. It's why "Columbus Day" is celebrated in the United States to recognize the "discovery" of America, even though North America was discovered thousands of years before by migrants from Siberia to Alaska. Ethnocentrism explains why white Australians celebrate the "founding" of Australia in 1788, even though numerous tribal groups trace their lineage back to ancestors who lived there some 40,000 years before the coming of the Europeans. It's why the Japanese first greeted shipwrecked European sailors as "barbarians" and promptly executed them. And it's why virtually every country that goes to war underestimates the courage, tenacity, and resources of their opponents, often assuming victory will come in a matter of weeks or months.

In some ways, a kind of ethnocentrism operates not only among societies, but often within them as well. In complex societies, dominant groups often act as though the cultural ideas they use to construct reality apply to everyone. Heterosexuals, for example, act as though they can assume everyone they encounter is also heterosexual and carry on conversations as though that were true. In similar ways, whites, Christians, men, and the middle class often act as though their outlooks and ways of life are at the center of the social universe and represent human experience in general. Most businesses in the United States, for example, routinely make little or no allowance for holidays not associated with being white, Christian, and of northern European background. This operates in the larger world as well. The routine use of "Have a Merry Christmas" in casual public talk reflects an assumption that everyone celebrates or values Christmas. Is a Jew, Buddhist, or atheist supposed to smile in return and say, "Thanks! Merry Christmas to you, too"? In this sense, every complex society includes a wide range of socially constructed realities, but some dominate and come to stand for the whole. The result is a kind of internal ethnocentrism in which diversity and difference are treated as invisible or, when acknowledged at all, as secondary and inferior.

The concept of ethnocentrism reveals how every culture limits the view of people who participate in it. But it also points to a basic paradox of culture and how we live and use it. "Ethnocentrism" is, after all, just a word and as such is a part of culture, the very thing it helps us see more clearly. In this sense, culture can take us in two directions at once. It can take us inward, into the limited space of our particular cultural box. But as tools for sociological practice, concepts like culture and ethnocentrism also point to the box itself and toward the powerful experience of imagining ourselves both inside and outside at the same time.

3

The Structures of Social Life

In 1971, I made my first trip to San Miguel de Allende, a small town nestled on a mountainside in central Mexico. After more than two years of graduate school, this was the closest I'd come to a real vacation—weeks with no responsibilities, day after day of long walks, good books to read, sleep whenever I wanted it, and freely taking in the smells, tastes, sights, and sounds of open-air markets, sunbaked adobe, and beautiful gardens.

After several weeks of this, I had a strange experience. For some reason that I no longer recall, I wanted to know what time it was and realized that I'd stopped wearing my watch. I knew it was afternoon and not evening, but beyond that I hadn't a clue. Since I hadn't been doing anything that required me to know the time, I'd lost my sense of it. At first, I was fascinated by this experience of "timelessness," but then I realized that I also didn't know what day it was, even after I sat for awhile trying to figure it out. This was a bit disturbing, as if I were lost, like taking a subway to the usual stop and coming up into a neighborhood I'd never seen before.

In a social sense, "lost" is just what I was. There are rhythms and cycles in life that seem natural and built-in to our experience as human beings. The passing of the seasons is one, as is the difference between night and day and the circadian rhythms that regulate when we feel drawn to sleep. But knowing the time of day by the clock isn't one of them. Clock time matters primarily because we use it to orient ourselves to what other people expect of us. It's a cultural creation and a purely arbitrary one at that. There is nothing in nature that corresponds to seconds, minutes, or hours. They are nothing more than a made-up set of categories. There's also nothing in nature that corresponds to weeks or the need to distinguish between a Monday and a Thursday or a Sunday. As a cultural creation, time is useful because it contributes to a sense of structure as we participate in social life.[1] I became "time lost" in the mountains of Mexico because I was no longer in a social situation where my daily rhythms depended on knowing the day or anything more than the roughest sense of the hour (and certainly not the minute). I was disconnected from time as part of a larger disconnection from my old social environment back at school in Ann Arbor, Michigan. I *felt* lost and disconnected because I hadn't yet adjusted to a new sense of structure in which time and day hardly mattered.

Like culture, the concept of structure is a key to sociological practice because it points to a great deal of what gives social life its familiar and predictable shape.[2] Cultural ideas shape how we think and feel as we participate in systems. Structure organizes those ideas into social relationships that connect people to one another and to systems as well as connecting entire systems to one another. When we go through a dramatic change in our lives—such as going to college or starting our first job or breaking up a long-term relationship—we often feel lost. This happens because we've changed our structural position in relation to one or more social systems. This means that we've also changed our connection to all the patterns of social life that go with it. When I was a high school senior, I knew what it meant to be who I was in that system; but when I went off to college, I didn't know for sure *where* I was socially or *who* I was in relation to things. The same is true of long-term relationships. "Partner" or "wife" or "husband" is a position that somehow anchors us. But with a breakup, all of that is gone and we experience not only a sense of loss, but of *being* lost because, in a sense, we are.

Social structure has two meanings. In the first sense, it's about how social relationships are organized at all levels of social life. We can look, for example, at how relationships connect individuals to one another as they participate in families and work. The relationships among members of a basketball team are part of the team's structure. Structural relationships can also be between whole systems, as between two competing teams or two nations in the world economy. The relationships have different kinds of structural characteristics that produce different kinds of consequences, which is why we're interested in them as part of sociological practice.

In the second sense, social structure refers to various kinds of distributions in social systems. In every system there are valued resources and rewards that are distributed in one way or another. In most industrial capitalist societies, for example, most of the wealth is owned by a small elite and the gap between them and everyone else is growing. The structural distribution of political power is also very unequal, even though cultural beliefs describe the political system as democratic. Another kind of structural distribution focuses on how people are distributed among the various positions found in systems. Most working people, for example, don't belong to labor unions and have jobs with relatively low levels of authority, autonomy, prestige, and income. Most college professors are tenured, and most of these are white and male; and only one person can be a national president or prime minister at a time. These are all structural distributions found in various systems.

In both of its meanings, the concept of structure can tell us a lot about how systems work and how we're connected to them.

Us and It: Statuses and Roles

We are always participating in one social system or another (often two or more at the same time). To see how that works, we begin with what connects us to them, which is an element of social structure known as a status. A status is a position in a system's structure, and we participate in a system by occupying one or more statuses in it. I participate in my college through the status of teacher, in the publishing industry through the status of author, and in corporations through the status of consultant. Note the difference between statuses as positions and the people who occupy them: we aren't them, and they aren't us. All kinds of people can and do occupy the same statuses I occupy, and the statuses exist whether anyone occupies them or not. It's true that statuses wouldn't amount to much if no one *ever* occupied them, but it's also true that they exist independently of being occupied by particular people at any given time. The game of Monopoly exists whether or not anyone plays it at the moment. In the same way, the U.S. Supreme Court exists as a system over and above the nine people who currently occupy the status of justice. If they all died in a plane crash, the court would still exist even though its key statuses were currently unoccupied.

The distinction between statuses and the people who occupy them is crucial for understanding how social life works. If we confuse the two, it's easy to make the mistake of trying to explain social phenomena solely in terms of individuals. Every time a U.S. president appoints a new Supreme Court justice, for example, there is speculation about how the candidate will vote on controversial issues such as abortion or civil rights. Legal scholars remind us, however, that people's opinions before going on the court often don't tell us much about how they'll vote in their new role. This is because the status of Supreme Court justice places powerful limits on anyone who occupies it, which new justices may not realize until they actually get there. There is a huge burden of responsibility that comes with being one of the nine most powerful judges in the entire country, whose decisions can shape the course of history. This is why the culture of the court places a high value on precedents set by past decisions and strongly discourages overturning them. Technically, justices can vote however they want; but in practice, they rarely feel free to do so because they feel limited by the responsibilities that go with being a Supreme Court justice.

This suggests that if we want to know how people will behave, we're in many ways better off knowing the statuses they occupy than their personal characteristics and intentions. When

U.S. voters elect a new president, for example, they often look for candidates who can change the direction of government policy, solve social problems, and transform the landscape of social life. Newly elected presidents often take office determined to change how things are done, but they soon realize that although their status is the most powerful in the entire political system, it's just one of many that make it work the way it does. While the electorate is quick to blame politicians for not delivering on their promises, they forget how much easier it is to put new people into systems than it is to change systems themselves. When the Clinton administration tried to overhaul the nation's health insurance system in 1993, for example, it ran into opposition from every side as the complexity of that system and the implications of changing it became apparent. Providing affordable health care for everyone wasn't simply a matter of what was good for people's health or of what the president wanted. It also had to accommodate a complex web of competing interests including insurance companies, physicians, businesses, labor unions, the elderly, the wealthy, middle class, and the poor. In the end, it became an exercise in frustration that satisfied no one except, perhaps, those who wanted things to stay as they were.

Heads of state may be among the most powerful officeholders in the world, but office*holders* are what they are. As such, when people are elected to such high office, they don't simply occupy a status. More importantly, the status they occupy is connected to a vast network of statuses both within and outside the government, and it is those *relationships* that limit what they can accomplish. The power of leaders to affect so many people is also what limits them, for every move they make produces a complex range of consequences that shape and limit the options from which they choose. No status *simply* empowers; it also constrains, in some ways *more* than it empowers.

What makes things still more complicated is that we participate in a variety of systems, which means we occupy many different statuses. Some statuses are ascribed to us at birth, such as race, gender, ethnicity, and family statuses such as "daughter." Others we achieve and occupy as we move through our lives. At school it's "student"; at work it's "clerk," "plumber," "lawyer," "manager," "teacher." We marry and become wives or husbands or live with someone as life partners or stay single; we have children and become parents. Notice that with ascribed and achieved statuses, we occupy the status whether we're actually *doing* it or not. I'm my father's son, for example, whether I'm actually interacting with him or not; and I'm a teacher even when I'm not with students. In this sense, we "carry" such statuses around with us all the time and are known by them, both to ourselves and to other people.

There are other statuses that we don't carry around with us because they only exist in a particular situation. When I step onto a sidewalk, for example, I occupy the status of pedestrian. As soon as I step off the sidewalk and onto a bus, I exit "pedestrian" and enter "bus passenger." With situational statuses, I have to be *doing* it at the moment in order to occupy it. Many statuses, then, have to do with both *who* and *where* I am in social terms, while others have to do simply with *where* I am and what I'm doing at the moment.

The point of occupying a status is that it connects us to social systems and provides us with paths of least resistance that shape how we experience and participate in those systems. It does this with a set of cultural ideas known as a role.[3] A role is a collection of beliefs, values, attitudes, and norms that apply to whoever occupies a particular status in relation to whoever occupies another status in the system. The role of teacher, for example, includes beliefs that supposedly describe who I am, such as the knowledge and credentials that people can assume I have. It also includes values that shape my choices, such as the importance of learning and growth; norms that regulate how I behave, such as those requiring me to attend faculty meetings or barring me from sexually harassing my students; and attitudes such as respect for students and taking them seriously. Notice that the status of teacher comes with several different roles, one for each of the other statuses in the system I'm related to. My role in relation to students is quite different from my role in relation to other teachers or to my dean or my students' parents. In each case I occupy the same status—college teacher—but the content of my role varies from one relationship to another.

Roles lay out paths of least resistance that shape how we appear and behave in countless ways. In schools and businesses, for example, people are often rewarded for having "the answer" to questions and often punished or denied rewards when they don't. This makes always coming up with an answer (whether or not you know what you're talking about) a path of least resistance for people in many different statuses. We could, of course, choose otherwise. I could say "I don't know" when my students ask a question, as they could when I ask them one. But, as an employee of a large corporation told me, "At work, it's not OK to say you don't know." The "not OK" is a form of resistance—a social consequence—that's built into the system itself through its statuses and roles. The resistance discourages us from taking some paths and choosing others instead.

Given how many statuses we occupy and all the roles that go

with them, it's easy to see how complicated social life can get when it presents us with more than one path at once. This creates the problem of role conflict, when the ideas of one role conflict with another's. When male teachers, for example, try to initiate sexual relationships with female students, the result is a role conflict that can severely compromise both roles.[4] For the teacher, it becomes impossible to treat her as he would any other student. For her, the conflict threatens her success not only within the narrow confines of school, but, especially for graduate students, the course of her entire career and life. If she refuses him, he can use his power to exclude or punish her academically. If she consents, she may benefit from some sort of favoritism for a while, but is always vulnerable to being undone by it. If others find out, she may be denigrated as merely "sleeping her way to the top"; or he may decide to use the power of his position against her if she displeases him or if he grows tired of her. Similar dynamics can operate in the workplace.[5]

From a structural perspective, sexual relationships between teachers and students cannot be equal because the roles that define their positions in the system are *inherently* unequal *and cannot be made equal*. His control over grades and other valued rewards, for example, is there for him to use whether he wants to or not; it's built into the system and the position he occupies in it. Given this, the two people involved may *think* the relationship is based on equality, but they have to pretend that they're somehow above the power of systems to define relationships and shape the people who participate in them. It may be possible for a healthy relationship to happen in spite of the profound conflict it can generate, but the odds are hugely against it, which is why many colleges and some businesses discourage or forbid such relationships. It's also why professional norms discourage doctors and therapists from having sexual relationships with patients, or lawyers with clients.

As part of sociological practice, this microlevel view of social structure shows how paths of least resistance shape how we appear and behave. It also points to the difference between what a system looks like and how people choose to participate in it. A role is just a collection of ideas, and there's no way to know exactly how people will behave in relation to them. Therapists and teachers aren't supposed to have sex with patients and students, but it's become increasingly apparent that many do anyway. Why? One reason is that we occupy many different statuses at once. The role of teacher, for example, isn't the only thing that determines whether a professor will initiate a sexual relationship with a student. The fact that the vast majority of sexual harassment and exploitation is perpetrated by men against women suggests something larger going on, especially when we see how prevalent this pattern is in all kinds of systems, from the workplace to the family. Whatever it is that explains why men—and so few women—violate norms governing the role of teacher won't be found simply by studying the teacher role and how colleges are organized as systems. We also have to look at gender as a status and the paths of least resistance that draw men to harass and exploit women in spite of what's expected of them as teachers.

The Personal and the Structural

Most of what we experience in our lives is connected to the structure of one system or another. At first glance, problems that seem to be just a matter of personality or human nature turn out to be at least partly structural, although it's easy to confuse the two. This happens most often with systems we know well, such as families. We experience them in such a personal and immediate way that it's easy to think that's all they amount to. My students, for example, routinely state as a matter of obvious fact that their families are "unique," which makes me ask why they use the same word—"family"—to refer to all these groups that have nothing in common. How is it, for all this uniqueness, that family life looks so remarkably similar from one household to another, such that we can almost always tell a "family" when we see one? Regardless of each family's idiosyncrasies, they're all families because they're a particular kind of social system that has characteristics that distinguish it from other kinds of systems.

Even if every family were unique, this wouldn't tell us much about the patterns that shape families—and our lives in them—in such recognizable ways. Nor can family "uniqueness" explain patterns we find among families—the effects of poverty and racism and divorce on family life, for example, or what difference it makes whether a family is based on a "marriage" that's heterosexual, lesbian, or gay or something larger and more communal. Even the most personal emotional problems are increasingly tied to how families work as systems. Many psychotherapists, for example, won't treat adolescent patients without also seeing the family, because they know individual troubles don't happen in a vacuum. Our inner emotional lives are never just that; they always happen in a social context.

Abuse in families, for example, is often explained in purely psychological terms. But this ignores research showing that people who abuse children, spouses, or the elderly don't have personalities that differ markedly from the rest of the adult population. Researchers of sexual violence, for example, have spent decades searching in vain for personality types that distinguish male perpetrators from "normal" men. Sexually, they seem to be pretty much like other men and stand out only with a slightly higher propensity toward violent behavior in general. The explanation behind "intimate violence" won't be found inside the heads and personalities of individuals, because the explanation is more cultural and structural than personal.[6] The simple fact that men account for most family violence and sexual exploitation is itself a structural fact of enormous significance. "Man," "husband," and "father" are social statuses that create paths of least resistance for the people who occupy them. That so many perpetrators of intimate violence occupy those statuses compels us to ask questions not so much about men as individuals and whether they're good or bad people, but more importantly about the systems they participate in that load the odds in favor of abusive behavior.

Movies, television, and other forms of popular culture, for example, routinely glorify the capacity for control and violence as key traits of "real men" and denigrate as "wimps" men who don't measure up. Even presidents worry about being seen as weak. Given this, we shouldn't be surprised to find men more likely than women to abuse partners and children. Abuse is especially likely from men who have more power than their wives in family decision making and from men who are unemployed and unable to measure up to the cultural standard of being "in charge" of the provider role. In households where abuse occurs, it's more likely to continue if the wife is financially dependent and can't afford to move out and support the children on her own. Dependence is compounded by the threat of violence itself: It's not uncommon for women to stay in abusive households because they've been threatened with even greater violence if they leave. What all of this amounts to is a systematic pattern of cultural values and structures of power in family systems that create paths of least resistance that make violence far more likely to occur. It suggests that family violence wouldn't be the epidemic that it currently is in the United States if we lived in a society that supported women's independence and gender equality, that valued the health and safety of women and children more than it does, and that didn't promote the capacity for control, domination, and violence as tests of manhood. This doesn't mean everything is society's fault and we shouldn't hold individuals accountable when they're abusive. But it does mean that if we want to change pervasive *patterns* of abusive behavior, we have to see how those patterns are connected to paths of least resistance *and* how people choose whether to follow them.

It also means that a social system can be organized in ways that promote destructive behavior that goes against important cultural values. Consider, for example, crimes such as theft, robbery, and drug dealing that people commit to get things they want. Are people who break the law participating in a society that actually promotes such behavior as a path of least resistance? Robert K. Merton's theory of deviance and opportunity structures responds with a clear "yes."[7] As Merton points out, capitalist industrial societies place a high value on accumulating possessions. The good life is portrayed as full of things, and shopping and buying are routinely offered as ways to feel better about ourselves and our lives. No matter what social class you belong to, it's impossible to escape the steady stream of advertising and its underlying message that getting what you don't have is the answer to just about everything.

Although everyone is exposed to the cultural value placed on possessions, the distribution of legitimate opportunities to *acquire* them is highly unequal. It takes well-paying jobs to afford many of the goods paraded before mass audiences, but most people don't have access to well-paying jobs. I live near Hartford, Connecticut, which is one of the poorest cities in the United States. For years there was a billboard near downtown that advertised Rolex watches, whose prices typically begin at well over a thousand dollars. I've always wondered how most residents of Hartford were supposed to see this ad in relation to themselves and their ability to pay. All kinds of people drove by that billboard every day and saw the message, "This is what you should have," but only a select few could actually follow through and buy one. The combination of shared values and an unequal distribution of opportunities makes people more similar in what they're encouraged to *want* than they are in their ability to *get* what they want in socially acceptable ways.

Being caught in this bind can produce a sense of strain and contradiction that people will try to resolve. One way is to work hard in legitimate ways—such as a job—to get what they're encouraged to want. Since the opportunity structure is unequal, however, this works only for a portion of the population since there aren't enough good jobs to go around. For everyone else, the choices are less appealing. One is to let go of the cultural value by deciding that possessions aren't so great after all. This is known in Aesop's fables as the "sour grapes" response: reject what you can't have. This is hard to do since we acquire values at an early age and they aren't easy to get rid of, especially when they're being promoted every time we open a magazine or turn on the television or radio. So, if we can't stop wanting things and we don't have access to legitimate ways to get them, then what? One answer is to come up with what Merton calls "innovative deviance": If the only way to get a Rolex (or feed my children or wear good clothes) is to break the law, then that's what I'll do. Another response is to rebel by challenging the system and its unequal distribution of opportunities. I might make revolution by demanding a good job for everyone and a redistribution of wealth. Or, I might drop out altogether and move to a cabin in the mountains and try to live off the land, rejecting both the pursuit of possessions and the "normal" life people live to get possessions without breaking the law.

The larger the gap is between the distribution of values and the distribution of legitimate opportunities for achieving them, the more likely deviance is to occur, whether as innovation, rebellion, or dropping out. This doesn't mean that high crime rates happen because people don't have what they need in some absolute sense. Instead, they happen because people don't have what others *around* them have and what their culture says they *should* have. If everyone in a community has the same standard of living, they tend to share values that are consistent with their common condition. But if a community has a poor population living next to a rich one, theft and other property crimes will be more common because values about wealth are shared but not opportunities to acquire it. This is exactly what researchers have found. One study, for example, found that rates of burglary and larceny are highest in cities that have the highest levels of income inequality, regardless of the absolute level of poverty.[8] So, communities with high levels of poverty where everyone's in pretty much the same boat will have less crime than communities where people are generally better off but some are much better off than others.

The distribution of values and the distribution of opportunities are characteristics of *systems,* not the individuals who participate in them. Students who cheat, for example, are in part responding to how schools are organized as systems. Most school cultures place a high value on grades but don't distribute legitimate ways to achieve them equally. How much encouragement and support students get from their teachers, for example, varies considerably by gender, race, ethnicity, and social class. In addition, students differ in how much time and energy they have available (especially when they have to work to support themselves). They also vary in the backgrounds they bring to school, resources available at home, and how much they've been able to develop their abilities and talents. Add to this the common practice of scaling grades so that a certain percentage of each class must do poorly in order to round out the low end of the curve. The result is a competitive system with paths of least resistance that motivate many students to cheat or to "lower the curve" by sabotaging the work of other students.

This doesn't tell us which students will cheat as a way to participate in this system. But it does tell us that we can be sure cheating will occur as a pattern of behavior because the system loads the odds in that direction. If I flip a fair coin, I can be confident that over the long run the pattern of results will be a roughly equal proportion of tails and heads. Knowing this, however, doesn't tell me what's going to happen on any given flip. In the same way, knowing how a social system works doesn't tell us how each person is going to participate in it, because sociological practice isn't about predicting individual behavior. It's about understanding how social circumstances shape patterns of behavior in one way or another, and the consequences that result. Sociologically, whether a particular student cheats or not isn't the point; that many cheat or only a few, or that it varies from one kind of school or one social group to another, is. Cheating in school and crime in society aren't problems because *this* person cheated or *that* person stole or *this* one wound up poor. What individuals do of course matters to us when it's us or someone we know. But that's not what alarms us about social problems like poverty, violence, and economic insecurity, which people consistently rank at the top of their concerns. What alarms us is that on some level we know these problems are rooted in systems we all participate in. As such, they can touch any of us at any time.

Structure as Relation

Statuses are important in the structure of social life not in themselves, but in the relationships that connect them to one another. In a sense, statuses are inherently relational in that they don't even exist *except* in relation to other statuses. You can't describe what a "manager," a "mother," or a "teacher" is without referring to some other status such as "employee" or "daughter" or "student." This is true of anything that indicates position and location. "New York" has no meaning by itself, but it does in relation to names of other places located by some direction and distance from it. If there was a community or civilization that lived entirely without awareness of anything beyond itself, naming it is probably the last thing people would think to do.

The relationships that link statuses—or entire systems—to one another are the main part of what we think of as social structure. To see how these are shaped as people participate in them is a key to sociological practice. Every system, for example, has a role structure that consists of a mix of statuses and role relationships. The simplest structure consists of the same two statuses in relation to each other, such as two partners in a lesbian marriage. A heterosexual marriage is more complex in that the two statuses are differentiated by gender into wife and husband and the wife's role in relation to her husband is culturally defined as different than his role in relation to her. In either case, a marriage system can change radically by adding just one more status— that of child—to the mix, as new parents know all too well. Adding a child to a heterosexual marriage adds not only that status, but also the statuses of mother and father. As a result, the role structure goes from two statuses to five and the number of role relationships goes from one to eight even though only three people participate in the system. Life suddenly becomes far more complex and causes familiar patterns of stress and confusion. A boy's father, for example, is also his mother's husband, and a wife's husband is also her child's father. In such a system, who people communicate with, who they pay attention to, whose needs they meet in a given moment, and how they feel about one another all emerge from a complex interplay of several paths of least resistance operating at once. Men's jealousy over the attention their wives (who are also mothers, but not theirs) pay to newborn children is the best known of these structural phenomena that happen so often because family structures often load the odds in that direction. If, instead, every household had numerous adults available for childcare, family dynamics would be very different than they are in typical two-adult nuclear families based on heterosexual marriage.

Family role structures can be complicated further by simply exchanging "stepparent" for birth parent. This happens in every family organized around a remarriage for one or both of the spouses. With children related to only one spouse, and related by birth to a parent who no longer lives in the household, the potential for conflict and bad feelings is enormous. Until stepparents develop their own place in this new family system, it's easy to feel left out and denied loyalty, affection, and respect from stepchildren. It's also easy for competition to develop over the attention and loyalty of the birth parent who feels torn between the children and the partner. Coalitions against the stepparent—children and their parent ganging up against the "newcomer"—are always a danger, especially when the children still hope to regain the missing birth parent.

None of this structural information tells us just what will happen in each individual family. It does, however, tell us a lot about built-in paths of least resistance and where they're likely to lead family dynamics when people follow them. When stepparents feel rejected and unwelcome by stepchildren, for example, they're bound to take it personally. But they might take comfort from knowing that the system's structure sets things up to go this way until a new structure emerges from the interactions of daily life, which are in turn shaped by how each member of the family chooses to participate in it.

We can do this kind of analysis on every social system from the smallest and simplest to the largest and most complex, from the flow of information in business and government to problems of command and control in the military; from the success or failure of social movements to the role structure in urban gangs; from the structure of international conflict and the global economy to the changing relations between doctors and patients in managed care health systems. The basic questions about how structure shapes social life remain the same. We can ask, for example, about the roles of industrial and nonindustrial societies in the world economy and how these lead to a widening gap between rich and poor nations and increased levels of inequality within them as well. We can also ask how those global dynamics affect the small scale of family life as corporations maximize their return on investment by closing factories and moving jobs from one place to another. Sociological practice always takes us toward the vital and difficult truth that everything is related in one way or another to everything else. It's what makes the practice so challenging. It's also what gives it such great promise.

Structure as Distribution: Who Gets What

As I mentioned earlier, the structure of heterosexual marriage is more complex than lesbian or gay marriage because of gender distinctions between wives and husbands. The difference doesn't stop here, however, because structure also refers to various kinds of distributions in systems. In most societies, for example, husbands tend to have more power and higher status, reflecting the privileged position of men in general in patriarchal societies. Like all social systems, families have resources and rewards that are distributed among the people who participate in them. The most important of these are power, income, wealth, and prestige, but they could include a variety of other things as well, such as parental attention or access to material culture such as cars. Whatever the resources and rewards are in a particular system, the basic structural questions remain of how unequal the distribution is, how that is accomplished, how the pattern of inequality is justified and maintained, and how this affects people and the system.

In most patriarchal societies, for example, boys are valued more than girls. In many societies, the birth of a boy is celebrated and the birth of a girl is greeted as a disappointment if not a catastrophe. Even in the United States, when people are asked which gender they'd prefer if they could have only one child, boys are still preferred over girls. In many cases, the higher cultural value placed on maleness translates into an unequal distribution of resources within the family. In China, for example, girl babies may be left to die after birth, or survive into childhood only to be sold off into marriage or prostitution. In nineteenth-century Ireland, the survival rate for girls was considerably below that of boys primarily because of how food and other resources were distributed in families. In many industrial societies, it's still common for families to concentrate educational spending on boys at the expense of girls, based on the argument that education isn't as important for girls.

Both within and among societies, patterns of social inequality are major features of how social systems work, whether based on social class, gender, race, ethnicity, age, or sexual orientation. At their heart is the distribution of power. Power is one of the most important concepts in sociological practice but also one of the most difficult to work with because there are so many ways to define it. The standard definition comes from the nineteenth-century German sociologist Max Weber, who is perhaps best known for his prophetic work on bureaucracy. Weber saw bureaucracy as a way of organizing and applying a particular kind of power, and he correctly predicted that it would become the dominant form of social organization in virtually every aspect of social life from school to religion to government.

Weber defined power as the ability to control events, resources, and people in spite of opposition, as a tool of control, coercion, and domination. Although this is certainly the form of power that's most valued in today's societies, it's not the only possibility. There is, for example, the power to cooperate and share or to nurture and facilitate processes that we don't control. Midwives play a powerful role in the birth process, but they don't control it or dominate the people involved in it. There is also the powerful experience of coming together with other people in religious and community rituals that affirm a sense of belonging and meaning in life. Related to this is spiritual power that often comes from deeply moving life experiences and forms of religious and other practice that people experience as extraordinarily powerful but not in a coercive or controlling sense. The human capacity to control, however, has been elevated to such a lofty position that "power" and "powerful" invariably look more like Weber's meaning than its alternatives. Given the fact that the world is largely organized around this form of power, and given the huge social consequences this produces—especially in the form of social oppression—it's easy to see why this definition is the one used most often in sociology.

As in so many aspects of sociological practice, it's always important to be aware of how inter-related everything is. Racism, for example, is one instance where unequal distributions merge with ascribed statuses to root oppression in the body itself, to make it a fact of birth as much as a fact of social life. Racism results in all kinds of structural inequalities, from huge gaps in income, wealth, prestige, and power to the lopsided distribution of workers across occupations. The structures of racism, in turn, are closely related to cultural ideologies—beliefs, values, norms, attitudes, and images that are the stuff of racial hatred and prejudice used to justify and shape patterns of race privilege. From this perspective, ending racism requires far more than changing people's attitudes, of getting people to tolerate or celebrate difference. On a deeper level, racism is woven into the warp and woof of an entire social fabric, and that can't be "rooted out" without changing the fabric—society—itself.

Systems and Systems: Family and Economy

Nothing in social life can be understood without seeing its connections to other aspects of social life. It's a principle that applies both within systems and among them. If you compare family life two centuries ago with family life today, for example, you'll find dramatic differences caused in part by equally dramatic changes in the organization of economic life.

Before the rise of industrial capitalism in the eighteenth and nineteenth centuries, most goods were produced within families primarily for their own use. People grew and raised much of what they ate, made everything from clothes to candles, and bartered for whatever else they needed. The same applied to most of what we think of as "services": What people couldn't do for themselves they did in common with neighbors—from raising barns to bringing in crops—or traded, service for service. Money played a small part; it was typically used to "settle accounts" at the end of the year when someone had done more for someone else than had been done for them.

Family power structures were patriarchal, with men's authority based primarily on their ownership of land and a culture that ranked them as morally and intellectually superior to women. In spite of this, what actually went on in families centered on women because they were responsible for most productive work, including raising children. Men monopolized certain areas of production such as the cultivation of fields, but most of the goods and services family members used and consumed—clothing, food, candles, soap, and the like—were produced by women. Women, then, occupied a contradictory position—subordinate in the power structure but indispensable in the role structure. To some degree, this strong interdependence between men and women may have dampened the effects of patriarchal domination, for most men needed women too much to take full advantage of their authority as heads of their families.

These family role structures also held an important place for children. Since most people lived on farms, children began working at an early age. When public schooling was introduced on a wide scale in the mid and late nineteenth century, the vacation calendar was organized around the family's need for child labor during the growing and harvest seasons, which is why schooling stopped for the summer. Since children routinely worked alongside parents and other adults, there was plenty of chance for interaction across generations, especially with fathers and mothers. While raising children was still primarily a mother's responsibility, with families living and working in the same place fathers also had opportunities to take an active role in their children's development.[9]

All of this changed with the rise of industrial capitalism, and the effects are still with us today. As people left farms to work in factories, living and working in the same place became increasingly a thing of the past. This created a dilemma for parents that had never existed before in human experience: They couldn't work and take care of their children at the same time. Many lower- and working-class families couldn't do without the earnings of both spouses, so children had to fend for themselves in many ways. But in the expanding middle of the class system, the dilemma was resolved by keeping wives at home while husbands went to work for wages. As is so often the case, the patterns found in the middle and upper classes became general cultural ideals, and working-class husbands and fathers increasingly measured their success by their ability to support their families without help and "keep" their wives and children at home. This is one reason why male workers demanded and won a "family wage" that allowed a man to support an entire family with his earnings. This was more than a concession to labor, for it also helped maintain men's dominant position in the family.[10]

Industrial capitalism, then, radically split the typical family's role structure. The productive work that women had done—from baking bread to making soap to weaving cloth—was rapidly taken over by industries that could do it faster and cheaper. This meant that for the first time, childcare became a full-time job for women, along with certain kinds of domestic work, such as cleaning. Increasingly, children spent most of their time with mothers, and husbands and wives no longer worked side by side.

Shifting production from home to factory also affected children's roles both in the family and elsewhere. Putting children to work in factories provided extra family income, but it also put children in competition with adults. This, along with concern for how easily children were exploited with long hours of work and poor wages under terrible conditions, resulted in legal bans on child labor with compulsory schooling in its place. As children lost their place in the adult work world, "adolescence" emerged as a period between childhood and adulthood. With it came dramatic changes in cultural views of young people. As children lost their economic value in families, for example, their "emotional" value to parents increased.[11] But children's dependent emotional attachment to parents wasn't—and still isn't—enough to replace an active productive role in family life. Until industrial capitalism transformed the world, children in every society were productive members of their families. When they lost this, they needed something to replace it in order to feel a sense of worth and belonging. The answer was an expanding peer culture isolated from the surrounding adult culture and often at odds with it. Adolescence has become a growing source of deviant and often violent behavior as adolescents reject mainstream cultural values. Adolescent males, for example, account for more criminal behavior than any other age group. As Margaret Mead argued in her classic study of adolescence in Samoa, such patterns may reflect the broad historical shifts in the structure of family and economic life and how these shifts deprived adolescents of a secure and meaningful place in society.[12]

Thus, in several ways industrial capitalism has undermined the position of both women and children. It has also affected men, although in different ways and degrees.[13] The shift of production out of the home and away from agriculture virtually destroyed the family as an economically productive group, at least as far as society and its rewards were concerned. What goes on in families is still critical to what goes on in the economy, since without families there would be no place for workers to be cared for and nurtured. There would also be no place for future workers to be raised into adulthood. But this contribution is rarely recognized as a form of productive work with economic value. Because of this, owning land and dominating the family no longer amounted to much as a basis for men's patriarchal authority. In other words, they were now the "heads" of something that had lost most of its importance as a source of status and power. The world was still patriarchal and organized in male-dominated, male-identified, and male-centered ways, but the position of individual men *within* that world shifted dramatically. Most men no longer had any authority over production— as they had on their farms or as independent artisans—but now worked for wages under conditions controlled by employers. This meant that men had to find other ways to secure gender privilege.

One answer was for men to control the wages they earned and the property that families purchased with those wages. It wasn't that long ago, for example, that women weren't allowed to own property, sign contracts, or spend the money they earned. Men, however, enjoyed an independence they hadn't known before. A capitalist economy based on wages allowed people to survive as individuals by earning money outside the family. This broke the powerful economic interdependency that had previously bound women, men, and children together in productive family units. Because male privilege allowed them to avoid taking care of children, men could—and did—take advantage of this possibility for independence in ways that women couldn't. Many people today believe this arrangement in which men work outside as family providers and women stay home and don't "work" is the natural way of organizing family life that has always been around in one way or another in every society. In fact, however, it is an extraordinarily recent social invention that didn't last very long, as the massive entry of wives, mothers, and other women into the paid labor force during the second half of this century shows.

In many ways, women are now completing a transformation of family role structures that men began more than a century ago. In this sense, working women don't represent a radical departure from traditional family life. Women have always worked in productive ways, and men were in fact the first to introduce the idea of parents working apart from their children. Working wives and mothers are part of a long-term adaptation by families to an industrial capitalist world that, like every society before it, requires most adults to work for money in order for families to survive. When men left the home for work during the capitalist industrial revolution, they created strains in family life, and women's exit is having similar effects, especially around childcare. This isn't simply because of the women's movement or because women now "choose" to work more than they did before. It is the direct result of an ongoing tension between economic and family structures, a tension that was first resolved—for awhile and in certain social classes—by keeping wives and mothers at home and financially dependent on their husbands. As wives and mothers move into paid work outside the home, the old ways of resolving that tension won't work, which is why there is a growing childcare crisis in the United States (except, perhaps, for families wealthy enough to hire women to take care of their children for them).

The ability of large numbers of adults to earn a living without being tied to a family system of production was unheard of before the capitalist industrial revolution. When such independence became possible, it changed the shape of family life and the relationships of women, men, and children to one another. As the United States nears the twenty-first century, the percentage of people who live alone and the percentages of men and women in their late twenties who've never married are increasing steadily on top of rapid increases during the preceding decades. Nonfamily households are being created at a rate twice that of family households.[14] At the same time, corporations are beginning to feel pressure to do something to relieve the strain felt by family members who must work. How all of this plays out will depend in large part on how willing we are to ask difficult questions about what families are and why they matter and about what an economic system is supposed to accomplish for the people who participate in it.

The Structure-Culture Connection

Concepts such as culture and social structure are tools, devices for thinking about social life in ways that help reveal how things work. They're useful because they focus attention on different aspects of reality so that, later on, we can reassemble them in our minds into a coherent whole. Because culture and structure have their own names and are typically discussed separately, it's easy to think of them as separate in reality as well—culture over here, structure over there. In fact, however, we never find one without the other. There's no such thing as a system with just values and no beliefs or a culture but no structure; every aspect of structure is connected to cultural symbols and ideas. In similar ways, systems exist only as people participate in them, and through this most of who we are as individuals emerges and takes shape. Everything in social life—from people to systems—exists only in relation to something else. It's easy to forget this, however, when we invent ways of thinking about such complex realities. It's like studying human anatomy: The text is divided into sections that focus separately on things like the nervous and circulatory systems. But these are somewhat arbitrary distinctions made for convenience, since nerves, vessels, and the body are completely bound up with one another. We can invent ways of thinking that allow us to *imagine* a circulatory or nervous system as something separate from everything else, but that's as close as we'll ever get to it. The same is true of the categories invented by most systems of thought, whether literary criticism, mathematics, or sociology. Understanding what culture and structure *are* is just the beginning, because we then have to see how they shape social life in relation to each other and the people who participate in it.

We can think of racial prejudice, for example, as a cultural attitude that combines stereotyped beliefs about different races and values that rank some as superior over others. People who don't qualify as "white" are viewed as inferior to those who do, and lighter skin is preferred over darker. Prejudice wouldn't be so much of a problem if it weren't connected to structural aspects of societies, especially role structures—who gets to do what—and the distribution of power, prestige, and other resources and rewards. Prejudice would cause little more than hurt feelings if it weren't for systematic patterns of inequality in economic and legal systems, in political power, in how children are treated in school and pedestrians on the street, in access to health care and all kinds of social services that affect the quality of life. In this sense, racism is not just a way of thinking or feeling. Racism is an integral part of the structure of entire social systems that privilege and empower some groups at the expense of others.

We can look at cultural prejudice as both a consequence and cause of structural inequality. Negative prejudice about blacks can help make treating blacks badly or simply allowing such treatment to go on unchallenged a path of least resistance for whites. But the effect also works in the other direction: If whites treat blacks badly as part of their racial privilege, they can use negative views of blacks to rationalize such behavior and make the privilege seem appropriate or not even privilege at all. This makes ending racism more than just a matter of changing habitual ways of thinking or feeling about race. It's also about a complex set of structural arrangements that shape systems of race privilege, and getting whites to give *these* up is a much larger task. If most blacks weren't concentrated in the lower and working classes, for example, they'd give middle-class whites much more competition over jobs and wouldn't be available to capitalist businesses as a source of cheap labor. It's unlikely that whites or capitalist enterprise would welcome *that* kind of racial progress. This makes it easier to focus on cultural prejudice as the sole problem rather than on the structures of race privilege and capitalist economics that prejudice supports. No matter how much we succeed at changing racism's cultural aspects, we'll still have to find a way to deal with its structure.[15]

Cultural and structural aspects of racism are connected not only in how they work, but also in their dynamics of change. Stereotyped beliefs about race, for example, are organized around real or imagined differences that are distorted and exaggerated to benefit one race at the expense of others. The beliefs are generalized to every member of the target group and are usually seen as inherent—people are the way they are simply because they belong to that racial group. Since the beliefs rarely describe actual people with any accuracy, the best way to undermine them is to give people a chance to experience people of different races and see what they're really like. This can't happen as long as people live and work in segregated communities. In the United States, for example, neighborhoods and schools are so segregated by race that a great majority of all students would have to move for the percentage of each racial group in schools to match their percentages in the population as a whole.[16]

Racial isolation makes it easy to perpetuate stereotypes because people never have to test them against reality. If we change the structure of race relations, however, by simply creating opportunities for people to work and study together, we make it easier for stereotypes to fall apart in the face of hard evidence about what people are really like.[17] In this way, integration lessens racial stereotyping and increases cross-race friendship, especially when people work together on teams and depend on one another to accomplish goals they have in common. This is one reason why the military and athletic teams have generally done a better job of dealing with racism than other systems.

The interplay between culture and structure is fundamental to social life. A shift in cultural values may prompt a shift in the structural distribution of power. At several points in the U.S. history of education, for example, the value placed on student autonomy and personal growth increased so much that the power structure in many schools shifted and gave students greater control over what they studied and how. Structural shifts can also stimulate cultural change. As recently as the 1960s, divorce was still considered a shameful state that could ruin a political career. As the number of divorced people grew, however, divorced people became more visible and divorce became more socially acceptable and therefore less of a liability. Similar cultural shifts are occurring around sexual orientation as gays and lesbians "come out" and increase their visibility as members of their communities, workplaces, schools, and places of worship.

Such patterns show how different aspects of social systems can reinforce one another, and how they can contradict one another and produce strain that changes paths of least resistance. Sexism, racism, heterosexism, and other forms of oppression continue in part because they conform to some powerful cultural ideas about the superiority of men, whites, and heterosexuals. However, they also violate other important cultural values about equal opportunity, fairness, tolerance, freedom, and respect for differences. This kind of contradiction has produced for the United States what Gunnar Myrdal called "an American Dilemma."[18] It forces people to confront the fact that a way of life that includes racism violates some of their own most cherished values. Martin Luther King and the civil rights movement used this contradiction as a powerful source of leverage during the 1950s and 1960s. Rather than calling on white society to simply *change* its values, they instead challenged whites to honor and live up to their *existing* values. This forced many whites into a choice between values such as fairness and equal opportunity on the one hand and the ongoing reality of racism on the other. As Myrdal predicted, the resulting tension continues to produce pressure for change.

The role of contradiction in social life was first seriously explored by Karl Marx who developed it into a major part of his analysis of how capitalism works as a system.[19] Capitalism is organized around a core set of relationships between (1) machinery, tools, factories, and other means of production; (2) those who own or control the means of production (capitalists and corporate managers); and (3) the workers who don't own the means of production but use them to produce wealth in return for wages. Capitalists profit from this arrangement by keeping for themselves a portion of the value that workers produce. Workers get what they need by holding onto as much of that value as they can. So, if workers produce five million dollars worth of goods over and above the cost of materials and other expenses, they only get to keep a portion of that value for themselves, with the rest going to capitalists.

Marx saw this arrangement as inherently contradictory. In the simplest sense, the interests of workers and capitalists conflict—each succeeds only at the expense of the other in what is essentially an exploitative relationship. In a related sense, capitalists are encouraged to keep as much for themselves as they can, since this is how they increase their wealth. But if they keep too much, workers won't have enough money to buy the goods they produce, which defeats the very purpose of the economic system and precipitates a crisis. In a third sense, capitalism is contradictory in its drive for economic "efficiency"—producing the most wealth for the lowest cost. In the typical capitalist society, efficiency is measured as the cost of producing each product (each car, each bushel of wheat) in terms of the number of hours of labor it requires. If efficiency improves, this means that workers are producing more each hour, *but without being paid proportionately more* as a result. Producing twice as much per hour, in other words, doesn't result in being paid twice as much.

The more efficient and productive workers are, the worse off they are in that their *share* of the total wealth they produce goes down. This explains in part what happened in the United States during the 1980s and 1990s: Productivity and corporate profits increased while workers' incomes stayed flat or actually declined as the overall level of social inequality increased. Between 1994 and 1995, for example, the median household income increased faster than the rate of inflation for the first time in six years, but was still below the average for 1989. When only employment earnings are counted, median earnings actually fell.[20]

From Marx's perspective, the only remedy for structural contradictions is to change the structure of capitalism itself—the relationships between workers, owners, and the means of production. But this threatens the major basis of privilege enjoyed by the capitalist class. Since the capitalist class has a great deal of social power and influence, the idea of changing the structure of capitalism runs into fierce opposition any time it's suggested. As a result, the contradictions are never resolved and the system is kept stable by other means, especially through the state. Early in the twentieth century, for example, the labor union movement ran into stiff and often violent opposition from employers. Federal and state governments often stepped in with troops and police to protect the private property rights of the owners of factories, trains, and other capital.

Intervention of this kind continues today, although in more subtle forms that rarely involve the use of force (except in emerging capitalist industrial societies such as South Korea). The state, for example, uses its resources to soften capitalism's negative consequences for workers with programs such as unemployment compensation, social security, welfare and medical benefits, low-interest mortgages, college loans, occupational safety regulations, and laws against unfair labor practices. All of these benefits are necessary because of consequences produced by capitalism. If workers kept more of the value of what they produce and full employment was a serious national goal, there would be less need for welfare and unemployment compensation. And if the profit motive underlying capitalism didn't encourage employers to cut costs, there would be less need for federal regulations to require businesses to spend money to ensure a safe environment for workers.

This kind of "counterbalancing" of one part of a system (such as the economy) by another (such as the state) can stabilize and perpetuate systems at all levels of social life. When a marriage is in trouble, for example, it's not unusual for couples to have a child in the belief that this will bring them closer together. In other words, they change the family's structure in order to keep it going. In more subtle ways, spouses may change the family role structure to compensate for a dysfunctional relationship. Children may be drawn into a situation in which a parent expects them to meet the parent's needs in inappropriate ways, in extreme cases sexually as well as emotionally. This kind of triangulation can continue for years as part of a family system in spite of the damage it does to the child. In each case— whether capitalist economics or the family—structural strain in one part of the system is connected to changes in another.

Systems within Systems

A lot of the focus on social structure centers on statuses as "parts" that make up systems. This is especially true of role relationships. But as the relationship between capitalism and the state shows, we can also look at what goes on *between* systems, where systems themselves are "parts" of still larger systems. To understand something like stress in families, for example, it makes sense to begin with the family itself. Families in industrial capitalist societies experience all kinds of stress and strain—worry about making ends meet, buying a home, sending children to college, getting good health care, taking care of children when both parents have to work, coping with emotional problems, the threat of divorce, and patterns of violence and abuse. Looking at the family as a system, we can ask how it works and how family members participate in ways that ease such problems or make them worse. The nuclear family, for example, is a structure that places a heavy burden on just two adults, a burden that wouldn't be nearly as hard to carry if it were spread out among many adults, as in extended family structures. On an individual level, whether or not men are willing to shoulder their share of responsibility for household work can make a huge difference in family life, beginning with the level of stress and strain on working wives and mothers and their relation to husbands and fathers. That choice, of course, is influenced by a larger culture in which male privilege exempts men from feeling such responsibilities, however willing they may be to "help out" when asked.

Since everything is always connected to other things, we can't understand what goes on inside families by looking *just* at families. We also have to see how the family and its members exist in relation to a larger world. The family survives in relation to an economic system in which goods and services are produced and distributed. When the economic system is organized to value profit above the welfare of people who participate in it, conflicting interests are built into the relation between economy and family. Investors don't buy corporate stock as a way to provide jobs for people who, in turn, can then support families and raise children. Investors invest to take surplus money and turn it into more money, and the most efficient way to do that under capitalism often results in a loss of jobs and dislocation and strain in families and communities. Family life is affected by forces far beyond the family itself when corporations lay off workers to make themselves more competitive and profitable in relation to other corporations, or when wages don't keep up with inflation and both spouses are forced to work outside the home. The stress that so many families experience isn't simply about the family, but also about the structured relations that connect the family to other systems.

This is true of every system. Towns and cities, for example, are related to one another, and to larger systems such as counties, states, provinces, and societies, and those relationships profoundly affect what goes on within them. We can't understand the crisis of U.S. inner cities without looking at the relationship between cities and suburbs. In many large cities, school systems are desperate for money, and student populations are overwhelmingly black and lower- and working-class. It's a combination that all but ensures continued inequality in education and training. Part of the problem is that funding for schools is done within communities, with each community responsible for its own schools. As middle-class people migrate to the suburbs, urban populations become increasingly impoverished and unable to provide for basic services, including education. One structural solution is to redraw school district lines in ways that spread the load of educating children more broadly. If school districts were based on counties or regions, for example, then a city and all of its suburbs would be considered one huge school district and funding would be spread evenly throughout. Where we draw the lines that define school districts is a matter of structural boundaries that define school districts in relation to political systems. It changes the definition of who's responsible for what, of what "we" means when we say things like "we're in this together," and of who's included in the responsibility to educate "our" children. And when boundaries determine how financial responsibility is distributed, they also touch on the structural distribution of wealth, which is a major reason why suburban communities resist broadening the boundaries of school districts.

Given the relation of systems to other systems, we need to expand the basic principle of sociological practice we began with in Chapter 1. Not only do individuals always participate in something larger than themselves, but those "somethings"—those systems—also exist in relation to something larger than *themselves*. To do this kind of work, it's important to think across the different levels on which social life happens, to see how groups are connected to organizations and communities, how organizations and communities are connected to societies, how societies are connected to one another, and how individuals participate in it all.

4

Population and Human Ecology: People, Space, and Place

Most sociologists see social life as primarily a matter of culture, social structure, and the interaction through which people participate. But this leaves out the fact that social life always happens some*place* and it always involves some number of people.

We could describe an office where people work, for example, as a social system consisting of beliefs, values, norms, a role structure, distributions of power and income, and so on. And we could look at how people use language and behavior to interact and make the office "happen" from one day to the next. Suppose the company "downsizes" its workforce and cuts the number of people working in the office by a third. What changes and how do we make sense of it? The system's structure is the same—the same roles to be performed and the same unequal distribution of power and rewards. The culture is also unchanged—same rules, same goals as before. What is different is the number of people who participate in the system and, as anyone who's survived corporate layoffs knows, the effects of this can be profound as fewer people must do the work once done by many more, and usually with no increase in compensation. They may feel lucky to have a job at all, but also question a management that seems to care more about the bottom line than about people who've been with the company for many years. This, in turn, can affect the entire system: Cynicism and resentment, for example, may emerge as attitudes in the worker subculture and affect how they perform their roles.

Numbers count, from the smallest levels of social life to the largest. Every teacher and student knows how much it matters whether a class has five students or five hundred, how difficult discussion is in the latter and how much pressure there is to participate in the former. And we are rapidly having to learn about the problems linked to an expanding global population, especially in parts of the world least equipped to clothe and feed the people who live there. Whether the numbers are figured in tens or in billions, we need tools to see how they affect social life and its consequences.

We also need ways to pay attention to the fact that systems and people don't exist in the abstract, but in a material world of space and objects. If five students in a seminar are seated around a small table, for example, the conversation will be much more productive than if they're scattered about an auditorium where they have to shout to be understood. If they're seated in a circle of chairs with no desks or tables to separate them, the conversation is likely to be more personal, which is why I often use this arrangement to talk about sensitive topics such as racism—I want students to be aware of how they feel as well as what they think. On a larger level, spatial arrangements matter just as profoundly. Racism, for example, depends on the physical segregation of different racial groups, an arrangement that reinforces the structure of race privilege and helps maintain racial stereotypes by minimizing contact across races. In this way, millions of people are literally "kept in their place."

Part of our relation to space and place is a matter of physical arrangements, from residential segregation to the placement of furniture in a meeting room. But that relation also has to do with how we use the materials found in physical environments, especially natural resources. A college classroom, for example, reflects a complex relationship between societies and natural environments, from using materials to make chalk boards and furniture, to drilling for oil to fire furnaces that heat classrooms, to using nuclear power to generate electricity to run computers and lighting. The classroom also reflects a world in which the system of production is so efficient that a small number of people grow enough food for everyone and millions of people can spend their days reading books and learning to think in new ways instead of working in fields of wheat and corn.

Social reality, in short, always includes a biological and material reality. Numbers count; space, place, and geography matter; people are born in numbers large and small and migrate from place to place; the stuff of the earth is transformed into the endless shapes and forms that humans are capable of giving it. This is the material reality of population and human ecology, and paying attention to it can inform and deepen almost every sort of sociological practice.

Human Ecology

At its core, social life revolves around people and social systems and the relationships among them. But those aren't the only relations that matter, for both exist in relation to a physical environment. Human ecology is the study of those relationships, and it figures in social life at every level.[1] In the colonial period of U.S. history, for example, the typical home was arranged around a single fireplace, which was the only source of heat. This naturally drew family members to one room during the winter months, which encouraged conversation, story-telling, and other ways of being together. With the invention of central heating, every room in the house was equally warm, which removed a major reason for people to spend time together on a regular basis. In similar ways, physical arrangements shape every social interaction. Office cubicles that lack doors and walls reaching to the ceiling, for example, make privacy impossible and signal a corresponding lack of status and power in an organization. This works as much at home as it does at work. In families, men are more likely than women to have rooms of their own (if there's a study or a workshop, it's more likely to be his than hers). As the late British novelist Virginia Woolf argued in A *Room of One's Own*, without a protected space in which to work, women writers could not develop their art, which is one reason why so few women have emerged as "great" writers.[2]

Every social situation has an ecological angle. Typical classrooms, for example, are arranged to reinforce the teacher's authority by facing students' chairs toward the front so that it's harder for them to interact with one another than with the teacher. In courtrooms and churches, judges and clergy are typically elevated above everyone else in a physical arrangement that underscores and reinforces differences in power and status. Both houses of the U.S. Congress are arranged much like large college lecture halls with leaders at the front on elevated platforms, an arrangement that both bows to the idea of hierarchy and makes spirited debate all but impossible. In the British House of Commons, by contrast, opposition parties are seated opposite one another in a relatively small and confined space, which makes face-to-face debate far more likely to occur.[3]

Ecology also figures in the arrangement of larger settings such as neighborhoods and communities. In comparison with cities in Europe and Latin America, the United States has relatively few public spaces like parks, squares, and sidewalk cafes where people can greet and socialize with one another outside their homes. Without such spaces, it becomes harder to sustain a sense of community, a sense of common ground on which to meet and feel the presence of other members of the community. Residential segregation by race, class, and ethnicity is another ecological aspect of many communities and societies that profoundly affects social life, especially in perpetuating inequality and oppression.[4] Physical separation makes it easier to maintain stereotypes; it leads to an unequal distribution of community services such as schools and police protection, and it gives a physical dimension to the unequal distribution of opportunities by separating working- and lower-class people from the better jobs, which are often located away from the central city. It also shapes patterns of behavior such as criminal victimization. Most violent crime in the United States, for example, is intra-racial because opportunities for physical contact are far more common within races than between them. Similar dynamics help explain why such a large percentage of violence happens within families and other intimate relationships rather than between strangers.

In this sense, then, every social system we participate in carries with it a sense of place and space (including the "cyberspace" that "contains" the Internet) and this shapes how we perceive and behave toward one another. In a larger sense, social systems also exist in relation to the Earth and the nonhuman species that inhabit it. To look at those relationships, ecologists use the concept of an ecosystem, which is defined by a given space and the species that live in it. The space can be defined in just about any way we like. We could think of a drop of pond water as an ecosystem, for example, or a chunk of soil in a field or the city of Toronto or the entire universe. Where we draw the line depends primarily on what we want to know about. Sociologically, what's most important to see is how human populations live in relation to one another and their physical surroundings, the consequences this produces, and for whom or what.

Ecologically, we're just like any other life form. We reproduce, live by using and consuming what's around us, and die. Like many species, we move around and build things. Just as caribou migrate with the seasons, people migrate to escape wars or find employment or get married; birds build nests, people build skyscrapers. We stand out in our ability to transform the Earth and our place in it in much more profound and drastic ways than other species. In addition to being the only species that cultivates its own food, for example, we may be the only one that systematically tries to kill off all its competitors for food. We also use technology to get around the natural conditions that otherwise limit population growth. For every other species, when there's too little food to go around, populations get smaller through higher death rates and lower birth rates. But most human cultures regard this as unacceptable, so they continue to reproduce and exploit natural resources with no limit in sight.[5] Other species, unable to respond and adapt with our kind of complex technology, are left to survive as best they can, which, to judge by the rate at which species are becoming extinct, is none too good.

In such ways, social systems profoundly affect ecosystems. But this also works in the other direction as ecosystems shape culture and social structure. The anthropologist Marvin Harris, for example, is a cultural materialist who argues that many aspects of human cultures come about as responses to material conditions in the natural environment. They are practical adaptations to the natural world even though they may not seem so. He tries to explain, for example, why the Hindu religion in India prohibits the eating of beef.[6] This is a cultural practice that seems irrational to many Westerners who see India as an impoverished country whose people need all the food they can get.

But Harris says just the opposite is true. Rice is the primary food grown in India, and the cow plays an important role in producing it. Rice grows in fields that are often under water, and the cow (unlike the horse) has a cloven hoof that doesn't get stuck by suction in the mud of the fields. Cows also produce dung that can serve many purposes, from fuel to fertilizer to bricks for building. So, in the simplest sense, the cow is an extraordinarily useful animal in India's agricultural economy; but this isn't enough to explain its sacred religious status. For that Harris looks to India's climate, which includes periodic and disastrous droughts and equally devastating famines. During these times, farm families who eat their cattle as a last resort will solve their food problem in the short run, but only by destroying what they'll need to cultivate crops when the rains return. What could be powerful enough to keep families from giving in to the temptation to eat their cows during such desperate times? Harris answers that India's culture protects the cow—and, therefore, the long-run welfare of India's people—by giving the cow a sacred status that no religious person dares violate.

What Westerners view as an irrational waste of animal protein is, from an ecological perspective, an intelligent adaptation to a difficult environment. We could apply similar reasoning to the heavy consumption of beef in the United States. Cultivating millions of acres to feed beef cattle is an inefficient use of land because only a portion of the nutrition in the plants that cattle eat actually winds up as food for people to eat. If that same land were used to cultivate crops that humans consumed directly (such as grains and beans), the result would be far more nutrition than beef provides. So far, the United States has been able to afford such high levels of inefficiency because a favorable climate supports huge agricultural surpluses. India's experience, however, suggests that as climates change—as they invariable do over long periods of time—the day may come when that's no longer true.

To a cultural materialist, every social system is shaped as it adapts to physical conditions in its environment. But as we've seen, this works both ways. Most species of life occupy very specialized places in the food chain. They eat only a few kinds of foods, and alter the environment (such as by building nests) in relatively small ways. By comparison, societies affect the environment in ways both huge and complex. People eat all kinds of food and change the shape and composition of the earth, air, and water in so many ways that it's impossible to keep track of them, much less understand the consequences they produce. Technology enables us to not only irrigate fields, build cities, and pollute the air, water, and soil, but also to alter genetic structures. Some cultures regard these abilities as part of a human destiny to rule or manage the earth; however, the complexity of ecosystems suggests that people have much less control than they might think. Humans have a much greater ability than other species to affect the environment, but we usually don't find out what we've done until after the fact. This means that we also have a much greater ability to do harm and damage and are the only ones in a position to prevent it. Only we can save us from ourselves.

Notice for a moment the language that's often used to talk about how societies affect the environment. Like all symbols, words like "harm" and "damage" reflect a particular cultural view of reality, in this case the reality of "nature" and our relation to it. To say that the environment is being "destroyed," for example, means that certain states of nature that are rated highly in cultural value systems are at risk. Those values, however, are not inherent in nature, but in human cultures. Ecosystems don't value one condition over another in that a lake full of fish is no less "natural" or desirable from the environment's point of view than is a lake full of algae. For that matter, nature also doesn't value humanity over any other species of life. Life is life. If we look at the vast majority of the Earth's 4.6 billion years of existence, ecosystems were dominated by what human cultures classify as "lower" life forms. As far as we know, over the first 2.6 billion years of Earth history there was no life at all, and for the next billion years nothing more than simple bacteria and algae. Single-cell protozoa appeared only 800 million years ago (after more than 80 percent of the Earth's history had already gone by), and multicelled blue-green algae colonies developed only 600 million years ago. What we think of as plants are only about 500 million years old, and mammals only 200 million years old. In short, the earth took the vast majority of its existence to go from a state of no life at all to what we'd call a swamp. Only in its most recent past—a blink of an eye in relative terms—has it started to look like what most of us think of as "nature."

If we take the long view, ecosystems can't be damaged or destroyed. They can change their characteristics, including the mix of different forms of life they can support (which may or may not include humans). They can change in how those different forms relate to and affect one another, as in which eats which. But the idea of damage and destruction assumes some ideal state, which is primarily a cultural invention. When we forget this—even in trying to "save" the environment—we're vulnerable to a kind of "species arrogance" that, ironically, is also at the root of the environmental "damage" so many people are alarmed about. In other words, it is a kind of arrogance to assume the right to do with the earth as we please; but it is also a kind of arrogance to assume the right to define what is or is not the ideal state of nature that should be preserved. In either case, we impose human values on a nonhuman world and usually do so without knowing it.

This doesn't mean we shouldn't act on those values, for as social beings we have to act in relation to *some* values, whatever they may be. But it does mean that those on every side of environmental issues have more in common with one another than they may think and face similar challenges in understanding their underlying assumptions about what they're doing. It is easy to forget that values are cultural and therefore human and not necessarily reflective of the rest of nature. And in such forgetting, it's easy to speak and act with a sense of righteous authority—whether in defense of jobs and human superiority or of the sanctity of ancient forests—that can make all sides sound disturbingly alike.

Making a Living

Each species of life occupies what ecologists call a "niche" in an ecosystem. A niche is a position, analogous to a status people occupy in a social system. As such, a niche locates a species in relation to other species and to the ecosystem as a whole. Where a species is located in the food chain—what it eats and what eats it—is an important aspect of its ecological niche as are other practices such as burrowing holes in the earth or building dams in streams. Through its niche, each species lives by using its environment in particular ways. This is as true for humans as it is for any other species. Hunter-gatherer societies, for example, use minimal technology and produce none of their food. Horticultural societies grow food in small gardens by using sticks to make holes in the ground for seeds. Agricultural societies use plows and draft animals to cultivate large fields. Industrial societies focus less on contact with raw materials—growing food, mining, lumbering—and more on manufacturing goods from them, especially through the use of machines. In postindustrial societies, providing services such as health care, insurance, and entertainment outweighs producing goods.

To understand human ways of making a living, we need to expand the concept of a niche to include the social relationships that organize productive work. In other words, we need to look at what Marx called a mode of production. In hunter-gatherer societies, people produce goods in ways that require cooperation, communal effort, and sharing. Capitalist industrial societies, however, are highly competitive, and wealth is distributed in very unequal ways. In horticultural societies, people own the tools and other means of production they use to produce a living; but in industrial capitalist societies, the elite own most means of production but don't use them to produce anything. Production is done by workers who make goods in exchange for wages without owning or controlling any part of the process. Such relationships—among people and between people and the means of production—are a crucial part of the mode of production in any society. They tell us a lot about how social life is organized and how it affects the people who participate in it.

Since the results of production are wealth and what people need to live, how production is organized profoundly affects people's lives, especially in the form of social inequality and oppression. As we look at the historical progression from hunter-gatherer societies to horticulture, agriculture, and industrial capitalism, systematic inequality emerges and grows, beginning with the subordination of women. Then comes class and other patterns of inequality of wealth and power: warfare, conquest, and empires; the state; institutionalized slavery and racism; and modern class systems and global inequality based on economic power. In the simplest sense, all of this became possible when people figured out how to produce a surplus of food, which supported larger populations and enabled more and more people to do something other than grow, gather, or hunt for food. This also made it possible for some to accumulate wealth and power at the expense of others and to defend their privilege with armies, police, servants, and institutions such as religion and the law whose purpose almost always included legitimizing the status quo. None of this *had* to happen as a result of increased production, but couldn't happen without it. Hunter-gatherer societies, for example, have very low levels of inequality based only on prestige, with honor going to those who perform important jobs well. Inequality can't very well be based on wealth in such societies, because they don't produce enough to accumulate and because survival requires a degree of sharing and cooperation that discourages competition and hoarding. They also have to move around so much in search of new food sources that it doesn't make much sense to accumulate wealth and then have to bring it along.

Changes in the mode of production are important because they create conditions that make other social changes more or less likely to occur. The ability to produce a surplus, for example, made rapid population growth, urbanization, and increasingly complex divisions of labor possible. These, in turn, made it easier for bureaucracy to emerge as a way to control it all. Historically, bureaucracy emerged in the West along with the industrial capitalist revolution, especially in the nineteenth century. But that's not the only way it came into being. China, for example, still isn't industrialized, but its government has been heavily bureaucratic for centuries. And although the most urbanized societies are industrial, many nonindustrial societies like India, Mexico, and Egypt are experiencing an explosion of urban populations.

Birth, Death, Migration:
Population and Social Life

In the simplest sense, since every social system happens only when people participate in it, to understand how social life works we have to pay attention to how many people there are, how they get there, and how and when they leave. Birth and migration are the two ways people enter a society, a family or a religion, for example, but migration is the only way to enter a workplace or a school (with few exceptions—such as kings and queens or the old Indian caste system—no one is born into a job). Too few people in a system can be just as much a problem as too many, or the wrong number in the wrong place at the wrong time (as anyone who's ever stood in an unemployment line knows).

How big a population is and how fast it grows or shrinks depends on a simple process of addition through births and in-migration and subtraction through deaths and out-migration. In most industrial societies, births are nearly balanced by deaths, and growth happens primarily through migration. In the United States, migration accounted for just 12 percent of population growth in 1950, compared with more than 32 percent today. The flow of undocumented immigrants has grown so rapidly that no one really knows just how many people cross the border each year, although government estimates range from 3.5 to 4 million.[7] At current rates, it's estimated that Spanish-speaking people will make up a majority of California's population early in the twenty-first century, a trend that has inspired intense debate over laws to control immigration both there and across the country.[8] In many parts of Europe—including Britain, France, and Germany—competition between foreign-born and native-born workers has been so great that social movements have emerged calling for the expulsion of immigrants.

In nonindustrial societies, which includes most of the world, growth occurs through a surplus of births over deaths. In the late 1990s, growth rates varied from highs of almost 3 percent in Afghanistan and Iran to lows of less than zero in Germany and Russia.[9] Three percent may seem like a small number, but not when figured into the laws of compound interest. At a 3 percent rate of increase, a population will double in around twenty-three years, quadruple in just forty-six years, and increase *eight-fold* in sixty-nine years, which is less than the human life span. The world's population is currently growing at about 1.5 percent per year, which implies a doubling from its current size of around six billion people to roughly twelve billion by 2030.

Population affects systems of all kinds, from households to the world economy. New households and families, for example, are created first through migration: People marry or otherwise decide to move in and live together. In some cultures, that migration requires the husband to move to live near the wife's family, while in others the pattern is just the opposite. In the latter case, the wife's already subordinate status in the marriage is reinforced by her physical isolation from kin who might support her, while in the former, the husband's dominance is lessened by the nearness of the wife's family. In societies where couples can live wherever they want, the problem is more likely to be a lack of contact and support from either family and the kind of isolation characteristic of the modern nuclear family.

The typical new family household starts with a population of two which is a relatively simple and manageable number. The best way to see this is to imagine what happens when we add just one more to make it three. If it's a baby, the consequence is a radical change in the household's role structure with the addition of several new statuses (mother, father, son, daughter, and so on). But from a population point of view, something else happens as well. With three people, coalitions become possible: Two can gang up against one; two can exclude the other. With just two people, neither can feel excluded because one person can't create a relationship to exclude the other from; but with three, two can form a subgroup within the larger group. Add a fourth member, and it becomes possible to have two subgroups, such as the children and the parents, and thereby two coalitions that can shape the distribution of power. Theoretically, children could organize in order to deal with the power of their parents, but it's more likely that one of the children will try to form a coalition with one or both parents to gain power in relation to the other child or parent. Whatever happens structurally, the range of possibilities varies with the number of people.

As families age, population continues to shape and reshape their culture and structure. As everyone gets older, for example, the age structure shifts upward and with it come profound changes in how the family works. Parents lose power as children gain autonomy and independence, and everyone's role expectations begin to change. When children migrate away to college, work, or households of their own, the shift in family power structures becomes even more pronounced, although financial dependence can preserve some aspects of it for a while. In fact, getting out from under parental authority is a major reason why young adult children long to migrate away and be out on their own. Physical separation also changes the communication and role structures and prompts the "empty nest" syndrome, which can occasion as much relief as grief. If daughters and sons form families of their own, the addition of new members to the network of extended kin both increases the overall family population and complicates most of its structural and cultural characteristics. At the other end of the life span, death brings not only loss and grief, but structural and cultural shifts. When our parents die, for example, we can find ourselves feeling as though now we're the true "adults" in the family, with no one in front of us to watch and measure ourselves by. This can be a time of shifting "weight" in family roles as we step into a sense of responsibility that we couldn't even imagine while our parents were alive.

All of these changes flow from the simple fact that how family life unfolds depends greatly on the dynamics of population through which people are added and subtracted, age, and move around in relation to one another. This is also true in societies and the world. This shows up in patterns of birth and death that reflect how birthing and dying always happen in relation to social systems. Although everyone has to die sometime, which statuses we occupy affect how long we're likely to live and what we're most likely to die of. Men, for example, are consistently more likely than women to die at any given age and from most causes of death. Some of this is undoubtedly due to biological factors since males are also more likely to die before they're even born. But a great deal of the sex differential in death is about sex as a social status. Men are far more likely than women to die from homicide, suicide, and accidents, as well as from physical causes such as cancer and heart disease that have clear links to how people live. Men are more likely than women to work at hazardous occupations, to take physical risks, and to act out aggressively. They're also less likely than women to see a doctor when they're not feeling well, which means they're less likely to find out about life-threatening conditions in time to do something about them. Men are also heavier users of cigarettes, alcohol, and addictive drugs.[10]

Death and dying have an especially powerful structural connection through the effects of social class and race. The wealthier people are, for example, the more likely they are to describe themselves as being in excellent health, a pattern that repeats itself with educational attainment and occupational prestige.[11] Death rates at each age of life are lowest among those with the most education and highest income. In comparison with whites, the death rate for African Americans is 60 percent higher, the infant mortality rate is twice as high, and life expectancy at birth is almost seven years shorter. For homicide, African American death rates are eight times higher for males and almost five times higher for females than for comparable whites. Suicide is the only major cause of death with lower rates among African Americans.[12]

None of these differences tell us what will happen to any specific person who participates in U.S. society, but they do reflect paths of least resistance that load the odds in different ways depending on who we are in social terms. Being a white man doesn't mean that I'll eventually kill myself; but it does mean that my position in the world makes suicide more likely for me than it does for blacks and white women. It also means that I'm far less likely to find myself in a situation where I'm likely to be murdered than I would if I were black. And being in the middle class means that I'm far less likely to work in dangerous occupations such as lumbering, trucking, mining, construction, or to be exposed to cancer-causing chemicals and other threats to my health. I'm also less likely to smoke cigarettes or abuse alcohol, and more likely to have health insurance and access to quality health care.

If we look at these differences from an individualistic perspective, we could conclude that they're simply a matter of personal choice: I choose not to smoke cigarettes, for example, and others could make the same choice. But applying the basic principle of sociological practice leads straight to the fact that every choice is made in relation to the systems we participate in. From there we have to ask how the paths of least resistance presented to people differ depending on what those systems are and who people are in relation to them. In my middle-class neighborhood, there are no billboards with glossy cigarette advertisements; but for many years in inner city neighborhoods across the United States, cigarette manufacturers have targeted lower- and working-class African Americans with ads that aggressively promote cigarette smoking as a glamorous and attractive thing to do, as one "pleasure" that's available even to people living in poverty. Which path is the easiest to follow—to smoke or not to smoke—depends to some extent on where you live, and where you live is invariably affected by social class and race.

Population and the Big Picture

If we look at population at the level of societies or the world as a whole, it's hard to miss the huge and growing mismatch between the needs and resources of societies on the one hand and the size and growth of populations on the other. The fifteen poorest countries of the world, for example, contain roughly half the world's population, and countries whose populations account for 80 percent of all the people in the world share less than a quarter of all the world's annual income. In many countries, per capita income levels have actually fallen in recent years and recurring periods of famine have become almost permanent facts of life.[13]

A common explanation of the widening gap between rich and poor nations is huge differences in birth and growth rates. There are, it is argued, simply too many people in countries like India, China, Mexico, and many parts of Africa, and their populations are growing too rapidly to keep up with the demand for basic services and resources such as food and drinkable water. With Mexico's population growing at a rate of 2.2 percent each year, its economy must grow 2.2 percent just to keep up without anything to spare to improve standards of living.[14] Since a 2.2 percent annual rate of economic growth is hard to achieve, it would seem that high rates of population growth virtually ensure continued deprivation and misery for most people in the world. What makes a bad situation worse is that high birth rates also result in a high percentage of children in the population, and children are relatively unproductive and claim resources that could otherwise be invested in economic growth. Also making matters worse is migration patterns that swell already crowded cities such as Mexico City and Bombay with unskilled workers looking for relief from rural poverty. What they find, however, are poor sanitation, not enough water, no jobs, and no roof over their heads.

The situation in such countries is so dire that it's easy to think of population as the most important determining factor in social life. But it's not that simple. What we call overpopulation isn't just a matter of resources being inadequate *because* there are too many people. Resources can also be inadequate because they are distributed in a way that gives a great deal to some and very little to others. China, for example, contains 21 percent of all the people in the world, but it consumes only 10 percent of all the energy used each year. By comparison, the United States has only 5 percent of the world's population but claims a 26 percent share of all the energy consumed.[15] Which society, then, places a greater population burden on the world? Which country shows the greatest mismatch between population and resources? Is it China with its billion people who consume very little? Or is it the United States with only a quarter as many people who consume five times as much? Or is it both?

If we look at the world as a social system, we can ask how population dynamics affect structural patterns of inequality between societies through which resources and wealth are distributed. It might be that there simply isn't enough wealth to go around. But it also might be that there is plenty of wealth that is kept from going around by a world system that gives enormous economic and political power to a tiny number of nations and the small fraction of the world's people who live in them. Certainly there are practical limits to population growth and size. The human species—within societies and in the world as a whole—cannot indefinitely ignore the natural laws that limit the populations of every other life form. But it would seem equally clear that wealthy countries cannot continue indefinitely to pretend that population is the only or even the primary issue shaping the fate of nonindustrial societies and that the solution to the misery of billions of people is simply for there to be fewer of them. The principle that we are always participating in something larger than ourselves applies as much to nations as it does to individuals. In that sense, the wealth of the industrial world and the pervasive poverty found everywhere else inevitably are connected to each other, and sociological practice is a powerful way to see just how this happens and why it matters.

A Complex World—A Simple Framework

Social life is infinitely complex, but the tools we need to observe and figure it out are not. This is true of many things. The millions of life forms found on the Earth and all the ways they're connected to and affect one another are also infinitely complex, but the basic concepts and tools of biology are not. We don't have to grasp the complexity of life in all its details to gain a working sense of what that complexity is about and how to explore and comprehend the pieces of it that interest us.

A clear and simple gateway to sociological practice lies through the basic principle that we're always participating in something larger than ourselves—social systems—and each system participates in something larger than *itself*. To understand how social life flows from this, we have to see how systems are put together and how they work, and how individuals choose to participate from one moment to the next. Because systems happen only when people participate in them, and because people's lives happen almost entirely in relation to systems, the connection between the two is profoundly dynamic. Nothing stays the same, even when it seems to. Systems are always being created and recreated through our participation in them—their cultures, their structural patterns, their ecological arrangements, their population dynamics. And, in important ways, *we* are always being created and recreated as social beings as we interact with people in relation to one system or another. All of this produces consequences, from our personalities to popular culture to the character of neighborhoods and communities to social oppression to the global economy.

Once through the gateway, there are many paths to follow. We can focus on large-scale questions about how systems work and the consequences they produce, or we can look at how individuals participate (as the following chapter shows), or we can blend the two in endless ways. Regardless of the path we follow, we take with us the basic framework for sociological practice that always reminds us of what the work and our lives are about.

5

Us, It, and Social Interaction

Having spent three chapters on those "things larger than ourselves" that we participate in, it's time to look more closely at the "we" and what our participation is all about. Social systems don't happen without us, and, in important ways, we don't happen without them. On the one hand, they lay out paths of least resistance, but we're the ones who perceive, interpret, and choose among them. We make visible and manifest whatever power they have to shape social life. On the other hand, we live as thinking, acting beings, and yet the stuff that thoughts are made of and the meaning our actions have make sense only in relation to culture and social structure.

Self: The We Who Participate

"Take care of yourself," a friend of mine says at the end of a recent conversation. As I return to this work, I wonder just what that means. Who or what is this "self" I'm supposed to take care of, and is the "I" who takes care of it something other than the "self" that gets taken care of? Is my "self" something I can touch, hear, or smell? I can sense my body and what it does, but my self is more than that. This is why behavioral psychologists like B. F. Skinner have little interest in the self: They can't figure out a way to observe it scientifically.[1] And yet, we think about the self as something real and thing-like that is responsible for what we do. When my "body" does something wrong—as when my hand takes something that doesn't belong to me—no one blames my body even though it did the deed. Nor do they blame my brain ("Bad brain!"), which directed my body to do it. They blame my self ("You should be ashamed of yourself"). Just exactly what that self is that I'm supposed to be ashamed of and where I'm likely to find it is an elusive thing, because more than anything the self is an *idea* we have about our own existence.[2] But it's a powerful idea because we don't live it as such: We act as though it's as real as anything we can see and touch.

Part of what makes the idea of the self so powerful is that it locates us in relation to other people and social systems. One answer to the question "Who am I?" is "Allan Griswold Johnson," three words that name me in the same way that words name an oak tree or a banana. They also serve a similar purpose. In my culture they identify me as male (Allan being regarded as a man's name) and thereby distinguish me from females; they distinguish me from all the people I'm not; and they connect me to kin marked by common names—Griswold being my mother's family name and Johnson my father's. A person's name, then, and the self that it names have a purely *relational* purpose of marking us in relation to others. The only reason to have a name is to be able to participate in social life, and this is

also why we develop ideas about the self in general and ourselves in particular.

As the philosopher and sociologist George Herbert Mead saw
it, we discover our "selves" as children through a process of discovering others and the ideas they have about themselves and
about us.[3] Infants tend to experience the world in an egocentric
way in that they can't distinguish between the world and themselves. Everything is just one big "whole" with them at the center of it all. This leaves them without a way to know that other
people exist as separate people with thoughts and feelings. As an
infant, I couldn't imagine that my mother had a point of view on
things, including me. I couldn't see that she thought about herself in relation to me and me in relation to her or about things
that had to do with neither at all. I could feel her body and otherwise sense what she did and said, but I had no way to know
that there was something going on beneath all that, that she had
ideas about who she was or who I was or about how to be a good
mother or what kind of man she hoped I'd grow up to be or what
to have for dinner. If I couldn't imagine that she had a point of
view on herself and the world, then I also couldn't imagine that
I had a point of view on things. As far as I could tell, the way I
heard and felt and otherwise sensed things was simply the way
things *were* and had nothing to do with who I was in relation to
them or how I interpreted them. I was like a baseball umpire
who, instead of saying, "I call 'em as I see 'em" or (confidently)
"I call 'em as they *are*," says, "*Until* I call 'em, they *aren't*."

I couldn't be aware that I had a point of view on things because I had no way to *think* about myself *as* a self, to imagine an
"Allan" who existed in the first place. Mead argued that we learn
to think about ourselves as selves by discovering the inner lives

of other people. We realize that other people think about us, perceive us in particular ways, expect things of us, have feelings about us, and have lives separate from our own that in many ways have nothing to do with us. This happens primarily when people use language to talk about themselves, about us, and everything else *they* experience as reality. They use language as a bridge of meaning to connect their experience to the experiences of other people. So, when I was hungry I might have experienced that simply as bodily discomfort, an empty feeling in my stomach that made me cry until it was taken care of. But when someone put words like "I'm hungry" to that experience, then I could imagine how they felt and put myself in their place. Without language, there's no way to be aware of that otherwise invisible realm known as the self, and without that, children have no way to construct their own ideas about who they are *as* selves. It's through language, then, that we discover the human *possibility* of a self by discovering what other people have done with that possibility. We become aware of our point of view *as* a point of view rather than as simply "the way things are."

Once we see this, we can construct all kinds of ideas about ourselves that make up the self. Because they are *about* the self, we use them to think about the self just as we'd think about someone else (as in, "How to be your own best friend"). We can talk to it, have feelings about it, evaluate and judge it, believe or not believe in it, defend or condemn it, scold or praise it, feel proud or ashamed of it, "get ahold" of it, disown it ("I'm not myself today"), lose it, be conscious of it ("self-conscious"), try to accept, understand, or "get over" it. We can say and do things to affect how other people perceive us and how they treat us as a result. We can wade into deep pools of paradox, thinking of ourselves as unique and separate from the world around us, even though "unique" is a cultural concept from that same world and the self exists only in relation to other selves. No wonder one of our most exhilarating experiences is when someone "believes" in us. And no wonder that one of the greatest crises we can experience happens when we stop "believing in ourselves" and feel lost, cut loose with nothing to hang onto. Note, however, that whether or not this is a crisis depends on the culture we live in. In many Asian cultures, thinking of the self as unique and separate from groups and society is neither a given nor an ideal of social life. In traditional Japanese culture, for example, it is a far greater crisis to lose a deep sense of attachment to the whole and be thrust from it into the uncertainties of individualism.

To participate as selves in social systems, we have to locate ourselves in relation to systems, to see how and where we connect to them and how this reflects back a sense of who we are. Most people don't know that "self" my friend told me to take care of. What they do know about me are statuses I occupy and the roles that go with them. At birth, we're known only by a handful of statuses—gender, race, age, and family position—because there isn't much else about us to know yet. As we grow up, we accumulate a social identity by occupying one status after another and using them to locate ourselves in relation to social systems and other people. As Erving Goffman points out, when we occupy a status, the role that goes with it provides us with a ready-made "self" that we can adopt as a path of least resistance toward acceptance by others.[4] In this sense, most people don't know much about who we are on the inside. What they "know" consists primarily of cultural images of the "typical" person who occupies this or that status—the typical girl, the typical student, the typical lawyer, the typical business manager. In social space, we aren't "who we are" in some absolute, objective sense. We are who people *think* we are, a reality of us they construct from cultural ideas before they ever know anything about us based on direct experience. Most people know very little about the "real me" as I experience myself. But anyone who thinks they know about fathers, men, heterosexuals, white people, writers, brothers, husbands, college professors, baby boomers, the middle-class, and people whose households include dogs, goats, and a snake may think they know quite a lot about me. What they actually know are paths of least resistance that go with statuses I occupy and the likelihood that I usually follow those paths. I may choose differently, but they can't know that unless they see how I actually participate in social life.

Not only do other people know us primarily through role relationships, but this is also a major way that we know ourselves. Think back for a moment to Mead's idea that we discover ourselves through first discovering others. If this is so, then it follows that how we see, evaluate, and feel about ourselves is shaped by the statuses we occupy. As we construct the ideas and feelings about who we are that constitute the self, we depend primarily on information that comes from outside ourselves.

These outside sources of information take the form of two kinds of "others." Significant others are specific people who act like mirrors, reflecting images back to us that we may incorporate into our sense of who we are.[5] "Significant" in this case doesn't mean "important" but instead means merely "specific." If a man in one of my diversity training groups comes up to me afterwards and tells me he thinks I did a great job (or a rotten one), he becomes a significant other for me because the information he gives comes from him as an individual. He also offers me a reflection of myself to consider as information that I may or may not include in my sense of who I am. This is known as the "looking-glass self": I use him as a mirror, and the reflection consists of what I *think* he thinks of me (which may or may not turn out to match how he actually sees me).[6]

Early in life, most information about ourselves comes from significant others such as family members and playmates. It's only later through a complex process of socialization that we develop enough to grasp what's called the "generalized other."[7] The generalized other isn't a specific person or even a group of people. It's our *perception* of how people *in general* view a social situation and the people who occupy different statuses within it. When I go to my physical therapist to get some help with my aching back, for example, I interact with someone I know as an individual. I know something about what she expects, what she's like as a person, and how she does things. This makes her a significant other to me. When I went to her for the first time, however, her name, gender, race, approximate age, and occupation were the only things I knew about her as an individual. How, then, did I know how to behave and how did she? Without knowing each other, we had to rely on cultural ideas about physical therapists and their patients and what goes on between them. Until we learned about each other as significant others, these generalized others were all we had to put together some idea of what the *situation* was about and who she and I were in it. In the beginning, we knew nothing about each other except the statuses we occupied and the social relationship between them. In other words, we knew each "other" only as generalized others.

What's makes the generalized other difficult for young children to grasp is that it's purely abstract. It's just a collection of ideas about status occupants. We learn what significant others expect from us by what they say and do, and children pick that up very quickly. But to distinguish between the specific woman who is my mother and "mothers" in general requires a level of cognitive ability that only develops as children mature.

The ideas that make up the generalized other are cultural, which leads us to assume we share their meaning with other people. Based on this, we also assume people will perceive, interpret, and evaluate us in certain ways when they know which statuses we occupy in a situation. This is why lesbians and gays are careful about revealing their sexual orientation to heterosexuals. It is also why heterosexuals feel no qualms at all about revealing theirs, to the extent that they don't experience it as "revealing" something at all, much less "coming out" or "admitting" they're heterosexual. It is why it matters what clothes we wear when we go out in public, because our choices shape who other people think we are. It is why racism and sexism and ableism (privileging physically able people over those who aren't) are so powerful. People think they know which status we occupy simply by looking at us and, as a result, easily associate us with ideas about who we are, what we can and can't do, and what we're worth. In this sense, we need to extend the idea introduced in Chapter 2 that we construct reality in a cultural sense, for it is also profoundly structural in relation to statuses, roles, and generalized others.

Since statuses and roles are elements of social systems, who we are—to ourselves and to other people—is profoundly rooted in our participation in these things larger than ourselves and the socialization process through which we learn how to participate. This makes understanding ourselves a basic part of sociological practice and not merely the province of psychology. Statuses and roles connect us to the social world and overlap our lives with other people's lives. They locate, identify, and anchor us in social space. Without them, we don't exist in a social sense, and without that, there isn't much left of what we know and experience as a self or a life. This can be a disturbing idea for people living in a culture that places such a high value on individual autonomy and uniqueness. But in fact, it doesn't diminish our worth as people; it simply means that we exist largely in relation to something larger, that we aren't the beginning and the end of things. Even rebels and iconoclasts who reject their society are organizing their sense of self and their lives in relation to something larger than themselves—the society they reject. And they occupy recognizable statuses within those societies, such as "rebel" and "iconoclast." In most U.S. high schools and colleges, for example, there are always a few students who play the role of the outlandish nonconformist who conforms to a cultural type by openly rejecting the idea of conforming to types.

None of this means that we're nothing more than statuses and roles. Not only can we make creative choices about how to participate in social systems, but there are all kinds of fundamental mysteries of human existence that are far more than social constructions. Every culture has *ideas* about such mysteries and about itself, but the best we can do with them is to construct reality second- or third-hand. Only in rare moments do we manage to shake ourselves loose from culture and experience the mysteries of life and death more directly. But that can be enough to remind us that however we construct our sense of social life and ourselves, there is mystery piled upon mystery beneath it. We aren't machines, and social systems aren't either. Both are far more complex, elusive, and interesting than that.

Self in Systems

The key to how we participate in systems is the concept of social interaction, and the key to that is the difference between action and behavior. Everything we do is a behavior, but only some behavior takes the form of action. A baby's first step, for example, is a behavior but not an action. A child's walking across the room in response to "Please come here," however, is both a behavior and an action. The difference? In the first case, the behavior involves no interpretation on her part. She doesn't consider the meaning of what she's doing (and not doing) and how her behavior will be perceived and interpreted by someone else. She doesn't consider it because she lacks the language and abstract cultural ideas necessary for thinking about what she's doing or what other people expect of her and make of what she does. In the second case, she can use language to anticipate what her behavior would mean to someone else, and can take this into account in choosing what to do. She can imagine alternatives and the most likely responses to each. In short, behavior based on meaning is action, and actions are the building blocks of our participation in social systems and social life as we interact with others.

On the level of individuals, social interaction is how systems happen, but it's also how *we* happen as social beings. As the late Erving Goffman put it in several fascinating books, we are like actors on a stage.[8] Every social situation has its props and setting, its script and opportunities for improvisation. And every play has an audience, except that in social life we are all actors and part of someone else's audience at the same time. We use a variety of techniques to have our performances seen as authentic, as worthy of whatever role we're playing, as convincing enough for us to be accepted in that situation for who we claim to be. So, we usually make an effort to show up looking the part, wearing the right clothes and attitude for that situation, knowing our lines, equipped with the right props. Like actors, we create impressions of who we are, what Goffman called "the presentation of self." Like every impression, the presentation of self is an ongoing process. It needs to be sustained and managed, especially when we do something that's "out of character" or otherwise calls our performance into question.

When two people go out on a date, for example, each spends time shaping the self they'll present to the other—choosing which clothes to wear, whether to shower or use deodorant or cologne, how to wear their hair, the use of jewelry and make-up. Every behavior contributes to the impression they create—what they say and how they say it; what they order in the restaurant and how they eat it; when, how, and how long they look at each other; what they laugh at and what they don't; how much they talk and how much they listen; if, how, and when they touch each other. When they part company, each is likely to wonder about the impression they made on the other, whether they said or did something that was misunderstood, taken to indicate something about the self that doesn't fit how they see themselves or would like to. Like players before an audience, as the curtain falls they wait for the response, the volume and duration of the applause, anything that might tell them how well their performance was accepted. On a date, it might be whether a kiss goodnight is forthcoming, or whether the "I had a great time" or "I'll call you" sounds sincere or merely polite (yet another way to manage impressions).

As in a play, both actors and audience in social life want everything to go as it's supposed to, because if it doesn't, it may compromise our own ability to play our roles effectively. Even as an audience for someone else's performance, we are never just that, for the audience has its role to play, too. This is why when actors in a theater forget their lines or otherwise ruin their performances, people in the audience often feel uncomfortable. The role of "witness to someone else's failed performance" is difficult to play because the mere fact of our sitting there and watching it happen contributes to the actor's pain. We become part of their failure, since if we weren't there—if there were no audience—the failure couldn't happen. And so we do what we can to protect the actor from failure. We don't call attention to the forgotten line, the stumble, the momentary lapse, the wooden delivery, but act as though it never happened, allowing the performance to continue with the hope that the people "on stage" will "get their act together." In doing this, we protect both them and ourselves as well as the integrity of the "play" in which we all participate. As both actors and audience, we have our own impressions to manage.

As actors, of course, there are many things we can do to protect our own performances. We can disown them with disclaimers such as "I'm not myself today" or "I was only kidding" or "I didn't mean it" or "I don't know what came over me." A man might say something sexist, but then distance himself from it by saying that it doesn't mean that *he* is sexist. Or, as Goffman points out, he might react with embarrassment that lets people know that his performance may have failed this time, but he's still committed to doing better next time.[9] His red face and awkwardness shows that he believes in the importance of what people expect of him. This protects him by reinforcing his claim to the part he has in the play.

Looking at social life as theater, it's easy to wonder if we have an authentic social self at all, if everything isn't just a cynical matter of figuring out how to make the best impression, protect performances, and play audience to someone else. The very idea of a "role" can seem to preclude the possibility of being authentic, as if creating impressions and trying to turn in acceptable performances invariably means faking it and wearing masks that conceal our "real" selves. But the line between who we are and how we participate in social life isn't as clear and neat as that interpretation makes it seem. To act as though it were invites all kinds of trouble. If we pretend that our role behavior somehow isn't connected to who we "really" are, for example, then we avoid taking responsibility not only for the role but for our portion of the play itself. Goffman argues that we are always being ourselves even though we may not feel comfortable owning up to the results and allowing them to shape how other people see us. If I play a role in a way that seems to contradict who I think I am, the person playing that role is still me and is no less real than the "me" who rejects this as not being the "real me." If I "fake it" and act in ways that don't reflect how I "really" feel, it is still me who does the faking, who appears and behaves in ways that create a particular impression. Whatever that performance is, it comes from somewhere in me, and if there is an unreality in it, it's in my not being aware of that simple fact and denying my connection to the consequences my behavior produces. As such, the problem of authenticity isn't that we're performing or managing impressions. The problem is that we don't embrace and own our actions for what they are as part of who we are. The problem isn't that we have so many roles to perform that can make us appear inconsistent or other than we'd like. The problem is that we don't integrate them with an ongoing awareness of the incredible complexity of ourselves and the social life we participate in.

Not seeing this sets us up to participate unknowingly in systems that produce bad consequences. At the same time, we cut ourselves off from our potential to do something about those consequences. When white people act in racist ways, for example, they often rush to make the point that they aren't racist. "I didn't mean it," they say, or "I misspoke," or "I made a mistake [by saying that] and I'm sorry." They almost never respond with something as simple as "I guess the racism in the world gets into all of our lives, including mine, and I'd better look at that to see what that means for me." In terms of impression management, everything said in self-defense is probably true: They didn't *intend* to say or do anything that would hurt someone or add racism to the impression people have of them. But this is beside the more important point that the racist content of social action is real, and if people choose—consciously or not—to be vehicles for its expression, this says something about the systems they participate in *and* about them as participants. In a racist society, talk and action that reflect and reinforce white privilege are paths of least resistance that tell us more about society than about ourselves. But the choices we make in relation to those paths tell us something about who we are in relation to them, and if we don't see that, we can't do anything about the paths or about ourselves.

Few things in sociological practice are as important or as tricky to grasp as the relationship between people and systems. In an individualistic society, the path of least resistance is to ignore systems altogether or to see them as menacing forces that threaten to swallow us up. The truth, however, is more complicated and interesting than that, and with far more potential for creative living. Our relationship to a system's culture is dynamic and alive, with us creating the world as much as we are created by and through it. We are objects of culture—described, valued, and limited by its ideas about who we are and how we ought to think, feel, and behave. We are also subjects of culture, the ones who believe, who value, who expect, who feel, who use, who write and talk and think and dream. We are creators of culture, part of an endless stream of human experience—sensing, interpreting, choosing, shaping, making. We're the ones who make culture our own so that we often can't tell the point where it leaves off and we begin, or if that point exists at all. We are recipients of culture, socialized and enculturated. We are the ones who internalize ideas, taking them inside ourselves where they shape how we participate in social life and thereby make it happen. And this thing we make happen is at the same time the cultural force that shapes us as we happen.

As a creative medium that we share with others, culture isn't us, but it also isn't completely external to us. It exists through us and we exist through it. It is *among* and *of* us. When we participate in it, it provides a way to participate in other people's lives. In this sense, there is no clear, fixed boundary that separates us from culture, and, therefore, no clear, fixed boundary that separate us from other people. Culture is like the air. It is everywhere, and we can't live without it. We can live without any particular culture, but not without *some* culture. Like the air, culture is always flowing in and out of us in ways that make it impossible to draw a true line between "I" or "us" and "it." It's both outside of us and in every cell of our bodies. As beings, we are *of* the air, but in a particular form that distinguishes us from dogs or ferns or bacteria. And since we all share this relationship with the air—as with culture—in a way we are all *of* one another—with the air and culture that you are part of flowing and mixing with the same air that inhabits me.

Culture provides ideas and materials to work with as we make ourselves and social life happen from one moment to the next; but we have to decide what to do with them. Culture isn't something that can think or decide or do anything; nor is any other aspect of social systems or the systems themselves. We aren't autonomous and independent in relation to culture; but we also aren't puppets on a string. We're somewhere in between in a far more creative place. We're like jazz improvisers who can't play without learning the basics of music. They have to know the difference between a sharp and a flat, major and minor, and how notes combine to make different kinds of chords. They have to know how to blend time, rhythm, and sound so they can shape the flow of the music and stay together while they play together. In other words, they need to know how cultural symbols and ideas define and underlie jazz as a musical form and how they shape the way musicians think and hear and imagine. But the cultural forms that limit them are also what they use to create, to bend and play with the "rules," to test the limits in ways that sound both familiar ("music," "jazz") and new.

This doesn't mean they can do whatever they want, even though jazz can sound that way, as if everyone's doing their own thing oblivious to everyone else. In fact, however, they are deeply aware of one another and the form within which they play all the while they're making it up as they go along. There is beneath the seeming creative disorder an unarticulated inner discipline based on a shared culture. This is what gives the entire piece its musical integrity and its *social* integrity as something happening not merely *within* individual musicians, but also *among* them. This ability to play within a form and yet improvise around and, at times, beyond it, is what gives jazz its unmistakable character. As with jazz and its musicians, so also with social life and us.

Making Systems Happen

Out of the interplay between us and systems, we happen, systems happen, and social life happens. In the simplest sense, social interaction consists of all the ways that people create and sustain a particular sense of reality. This works through both action and appearance. If employees in a bank, for example, dressed in clown costumes and gorilla suits, customers would have a hard time identifying this as a bank where they can confidently deposit their hard earned money. Appearance and action mirror each other. The hushed atmosphere in a typical bank and the quiet, efficient way that tellers handle transactions sustain the shared sense that this is a serious place where your money will be well taken care of. People don't laugh a lot in banks, or make jokes about bank failures or embezzlement, just as airline pilots and flight attendants don't make funny remarks about

crashes or bombs. In fact, in the United States it's a criminal of-
fense to make jokes about possibly carrying a bomb onto a plane.
This is because the shared sense that flying is a safe way to travel
is a fragile social reality that can be sustained only by controlling
anything that people might say or do to indicate otherwise. As I
sit in my seat at 30,000 feet, reading a book or eating lunch, I
usually don't realize how fine a line separates the alternate realities of safety and immanent danger, and everything around me
is designed to encourage me not to. The comfort of the seats, the
availability of movies, food, reading material, music, air conditioning, heat, telephones—all create a sense of reality that, when
I consider where all of this is taking place, is in some ways absurd.
But I accept it and make it "normal" and unremarkable until
something goes wrong to suggest otherwise.

Every social situation is defined by a reality that exists only
as people actively shape and support it.[10] In something as simple
as a conversation, we have to engage in a kind of dance of ges-
tures, talk, and body language to sustain a shared sense that this
thing we call a "conversation" is in fact happening from one moment to the next. There are all kinds of methods, for example,
that we can use to assure someone that we're paying attention to
what they're saying. We look at them, nod our heads now and
then, murmur an occasional "uh huh," smile or laugh at the
funny parts, frown at something serious, ask a question or make
a comment that's related to what they've said. Without that, the
idea that a conversation is happening can't be sustained as a
shared reality. I've done a workshop exercise where people pair
off and one person tells a story to the other while the partner pre-
tends to be completely oblivious to what's being said (sometimes going to sleep). It's an awful experience for the speaker

who typically can't think of what to say next or can but can't get their mouths to say it. In this sense, "having a conversation" is a reality that we create and sustain between us, and everything we do or don't do figures into making that happen. The methods are something we have to learn, and they vary from one culture to another. In some cultures, for example, a sign of paying attention in a conversation is looking at the other person's eyes from time to time. In other cultures, however, this is considered a sign of disrespect if done by someone lower in authority toward someone higher. So, when typical middle-class white teachers in U.S. schools try to have a conversation with students from any number of Hispanic or Asian cultures, they find their students seeming to shirk their responsibility to help keep the conversation going (thinking, perhaps, they're trying to conceal some wrongdoing), when what's really going on is a show of respect and politeness. What sustains a conversation in one culture can have just the opposite effect in another.

We continually use our knowledge of how reality is constructed to figure out from one moment to the next what's going on and how to do our part to keep it going. At the movies, for example, I walk up to the theater and notice a line of people extending out the front door and down the sidewalk. I take this to mean that they haven't started selling tickets for the next show, and I'm supposed to go to the end of the line and wait for it to move. The social reality of a waiting line is a fragile one, because most people would rather be at the front than farther back. It's so fragile that it takes very little to undo it. It takes only a few people to leave the line and go into the door ahead of everyone else for people to start doubting that it is in fact a "line" in which the rules of staying in place and waiting your turn apply. When this happens, the line can literally fall apart physically and as a shared social reality, which depends on certain patterns of social action to maintain a consensus that it exists.

Because the methods we use to sustain a social reality are used over and over again, they often take on a ritual quality.[11] Intimate relations between life partners, for example, are usually based on the assumption that the two people love each other. Since an assumption is just an idea, it is sustained through rituals that call attention to it as part of the reality these two people participate in day after day. Such rituals might include saying goodnight before going to sleep, perhaps accompanied with a kiss, or saying "I love you" before ending a phone conversation, or kissing as part of saying goodbye when going off in separate directions at the start of a workday. We may not think of such rituals as sustaining reality until our partner fails to enact them, especially over a period of time. In itself, each "I love you," each kiss or "goodnight" doesn't amount to much; but as part of a fabric that holds together the social reality of a love relationship, it can take on much greater significance. It may not take many lapses to raise insecurity in a partner, worry that something is wrong in the relationship, that the assumption of love and commitment is weaker than it was. Like many aspects of interaction ritual, we don't even know they're there until someone deviates from them and we notice the hole in the social fabric that marks where they're supposed to be.

With sociological practice, focusing on interaction naturally draws us toward individuals, but it's important to keep in mind that almost everything we say or do happens in relation to one social system or another. What goes on among people is rarely just a matter of that, but often has implications for larger systems even though we don't know it at the time. Linguist Deborah Tannen has written several books on how women and men talk to one another.[12] She notices that men tend to talk in ways that enhance their status—they're more likely than women to interrupt during conversations, to use aggressive language and tones of voice, and to avoid doing anything that might suggest a lack of control such as asking for directions or saying they don't know the answer to a question. Women, on the other hand, are more likely than men to interact in ways that support personal relationships—to listen attentively while others talk, to wait their turn rather than interrupt, to avoid verbal aggression, and to be more open about their doubts. Tannen explains these patterns as a relatively simple matter of children playing in same-sex groups as they grow up, thereby socialized by their peers to interact in different ways. They grow up in what amounts to different cultures, Tannen argues, and behave accordingly.

The problem with Tannen's approach is that she never links such differences to the larger social context that encourages them. She tells us that a boy learns to interact aggressively by hanging out with other boys, but she doesn't tell us where *those* boys learn to interact aggressively. It's as if boys and girls invent different patterns spontaneously and all by themselves, rather than learning them as part of their socialization into the larger society they *both* inhabit. More importantly, Tannen doesn't ask what kind of society would have paths of least resistance that lead men to seek status and women to attend more to personal relationships. She barely mentions that we live in a society that is male-dominated, male-identified, and male-centered. In such a world, men who seek status and women who attend to personal relationships also reinforce male gender privilege and the price women pay for it. When women and men interact along their paths of least resistance, they do more than talk differently. They also play a part in making a particular kind of society happen from one moment to the next. When men interrupt and women don't object, when men answer questions even when they don't know and women remain silent or say they don't know, when men argue aggressively for their point of view and women raise questions and otherwise show an openness to alternatives—this is how gender privilege *happens* to shape a major structural feature of society as a whole, with all the systems—from family to the workplace—included in it.

This is true of every form of social inequality whose patterns of inclusion and exclusion, advantage and disadvantage, reward and punishment all contribute to privileging some groups over others. In all kinds of workplaces, for example, white women, people of color, Asians, gays, lesbians, and bisexuals find themselves at the receiving end of messages that make them feel like unwelcome outsiders. Sometimes it's overt and deliberate, but often it's woven into the everyday fabric of interaction. As Rosabeth Moss Kanter observed about corporations, when men use strong language in the presence of women, they typically apologize to the women.[13] While the men may think they're simply being sensitive or polite, they're also sending the message that if the women weren't there, the men wouldn't have to pay such close attention to how they talk. By apologizing, they draw attention to the exceptional nature of women's presence and identify them as outsiders who interfere with the normal flow of conversation.

Gays and lesbians experience this kind of exclusion all the time in the form of an ongoing assumption by heterosexuals that everyone else is heterosexual, too.[14] Since "coming out" carries all kinds of risks at work, gays and lesbians have to be careful in the simplest everyday interactions, such as Monday morning talk about what coworkers did over the weekend. When heterosexuals try to imagine telling someone all about their family without ever using a word that indicates anyone's gender, they get some idea of what it's like to be gay or lesbian in the workplace. A heterosexual has nothing to lose by casually "revealing" a partner's gender, as when a woman refers to her partner as "he." But a lesbian who does the same thing could find herself in a great deal of trouble, excluded if not harassed and discriminated against in ways that threaten her livelihood. Since heterosexuals have much greater freedom to talk about their personal lives, such talk becomes a form of privilege because it is denied to others.[15] Heterosexuals are rarely aware of this, which is also part of their privilege.

In a society that privileges whites, people of many races must deal with patterns of interaction that exclude and discriminate. The messages "you aren't white" and "you don't belong here" are sent routinely and in a variety of ways. Black men, for example, are routinely treated as objects of fear in public places as white people hug packages and bags more tightly against their bodies as they pass by or avoid the encounter by crossing the street. Blacks often have their presence challenged, however politely. A black partner in a large law firm, for example, comes to work early one morning and is confronted by a young newly hired white attorney who doesn't know who he's talking to. "Can I help you?" the young man asks pointedly. When told "No," he repeats the question until the senior lawyer angrily explains who he is. A black U.S. federal judge tells the story of waiting for a cab with several colleagues—all dressed in suits and ties—outside a prominent hotel in a major city. A white woman drove up in her car, got out, and handed the judge her keys as she strode into the hotel.[16]

It is in such ways that "large" structures of social inequality which characterize entire societies play themselves out in everyday life. The countless ways that such systems limit and damage people's lives don't usually take the form of overt and deliberate harm. Instead, they happen through a particular choice of words, a tone of voice, the timing of a silence or an averted gaze, a seemingly innocent question. This often makes it especially difficult for members of dominant, privileged groups to appreciate that their privilege even exists, not to mention what a cost it exacts from others. And this is what makes it especially difficult for members of subordinate groups to endure the small everyday exclusions and insults, no one of which carries great weight, but that accumulate into the kind of burden that gives oppression its name.

The interplay between the details of speech, gesture, and behavior on the one hand and how social systems happen on the other operates in some way at every level and in every realm of social life. It gives significance to everything we do and don't do, and to the choices that shape how we do it. It is, ultimately, what connects us to a social reality larger than ourselves and our own experience, a reality shaped through our participation which, at the same time, shapes who we are.

6

Living the Practice
and the Promise

Sociology isn't simply a field of study, a discipline, an intellectual pursuit; it's also a form of practice, a way of living in the world. As such, it changes how we see the world and how we experience it, which is a first step toward new ways of participating in it.

Sociology as life and practice can affect us in many ways. The more we practice, the more we notice the assumptions and understandings that underlie everyday life. They are rarely spoken or otherwise made explicit, but they operate in powerful ways to shape how we perceive reality, how we feel, and how we behave. The practice also takes us toward a deeper understanding of larger social issues and problems, where they come from, and what they have to do with us. This isn't to justify blame, but to clarify the choices we make every day as we participate in social life, and our potential to be part of the solution rather than merely part of the problem. If systems and their consequences are continually created and recreated, and if this happens only through the participation of individuals, then the possibilities for making a difference are endless and simply wait for us to notice and act on them.

Sociology as life and practice can take us deeper on every level of human experience. To provide a clearer sense of this, consider four questions: What does "I love you" really mean? Why don't people vote in the United States? Why is there poverty? And who are we *really*?

What Does "I Love You" Really Mean?

To most of us, words and language are little more than a way to label the world, to represent symbolically what we perceive, feel, and think and to communicate it to other people. It is much more than that, however, for as we saw in Chapter 2, it is also a shared medium for creating a sense of reality in each social situation. As such, it acts as a powerful glue that holds social systems and our participation in them together. It allows us to assume basic outlines of what's real and what's not, without which social life simply couldn't happen.

Of all the ways we use language, one of the most intriguing and least studied is performative language. These are expressions that count as actions in and of themselves. We often use language to describe what we've done, are doing, or intend to do, but while the words have meaning, the saying of them isn't a social action. I might say, for example, "I've been thinking about quitting my job," but that isn't doing anything except saying some words to communicate what I think. If I go to my employer, however, and say, "I quit," I haven't just said words that convey some meaning. I've also *done* something: I've actually quit my job and in that changed a piece of social reality—my relation to my employer.

This is what makes performative language *performative*: the words aren't just *about* behavior, they *are* a meaningful action. They are an action because the content of what is said is regarded as action beyond the mechanics of talk. In the same way, when I say, "I promise to pay you the money I owe," I don't just communicate my intentions. I also *do* something by saying words that actually change my relationship to the person I'm speaking to. The words invoke a set of social expectations that bind me to certain actions and give others the right to hold me accountable to them. To say "I promise" *is* to promise and has consequences that are no less concrete than any other social action. This is true for any kind of oath, from swearing to tell the truth in a court of law to swearing loyalty to a government.

Probably the best known example of performative language is the "I do" spoken by people in the act of marriage. It's no accident that these two simple words are so often a source of humor in movies as the audience waits breathlessly while a character stands there in silence, hesitating, holding onto the potential *not* to say them. All of the other words in a marriage ceremony amount to nothing without these two. When spoken at the right moment, they have the social authority to transform the relationship between two people and their families and between them and institutions such as the state, whose approval is necessary to undo the effects of saying them. The words actually change the structure of relationships.

It's relatively easy to see how "I promise" and "I quit" qualify as performative language, but a more interesting case is performative language that doesn't stand out quite so clearly. When I say, "I'm sorry," for example, I could simply be expressing sorrow for someone else's loss or pain, whether or not I had anything to do with causing it. The words could serve, however, as performative language that alters my relationship with someone else. If I hurt someone by being insensitive to their feelings, I incur a social obligation to accept their anger because they have a right to it. I'm also obliged to at least try to make it up to them in some way. One way to escape the anger and the obligation—to return the relationship to the way it was before—is to use "I'm sorry" as performative language that gets me off the hook. I hurt his feelings and he gets angry and I say, "I'm sorry." He persists in his anger and I ward him off with "I said I was sorry, didn't I?" If the words simply expressed my feelings, they would have relatively little effect ("You may feel sorry, but I'm still hurt"). But as performative language, they can alter the relationship itself if he no longer feels he has the right to continue being angry.

This kind of performative language is powerful because we're unaware that it's performative. "I love you" may be the single most potent (and dangerous) bit of hidden performative language there is. Since the emergence of romantic love in the European age of chivalry, "I love you" has become one of the most important phrases people hope to hear or have occasion to say. Especially in Western societies (but increasingly elsewhere as well), there seems to be an obsession with love—getting it, having it, keeping it, and recovering from the loss of it. Love is everywhere, from literature and film to music, art, and the corridors of every high school. There seem to be few things in our lives that have as much power to shape our sense of well-being or our willingness to take risks that might make us look like fools as the quest to hear those three short words spoken by the right person at the right time.

What, then, do the words mean? In the simplest sense, they work like any other words to communicate information, except in this case the information takes on a high cultural value. The words form a message about how one person perceives and feels about another. If this were all that "I love you" was about, then we'd expect that everyone would want to hear them as much as possible, especially in societies where people are obsessed with loving and being loved. But, this isn't the case, for the "wrong" person saying "I love you" can be just as much a problem as the "right" person *not* saying it. Saying (and not saying) "I love you" is so problematic because the words do much more than communicate information about reality. They also play a key performative role in altering reality. This is why those three little words are the source of so much attention and trouble.

We could, for example, see "I love you" as a gift of sorts, like a compliment. If we follow the norm of reciprocity, we feel obliged to complete the exchange by replying in kind ("I love you." "I love you, too.").[1] We could also interpret it as a way of showing vulnerability, of taking the risk of exposing our feelings to someone else in order to deepen our relationship. As with a gift, this also calls upon the other person to reciprocate in some way. In either case, then, when we tell people that we love them—especially for the first time—we are hoping, if not expecting, that they'll tell us they love us, too. If the words have gone back and forth between us over a long period, we might assume the response even if it isn't actually spoken. But otherwise, if the reply falls short of "I love you, too," we have a problem. Responses like "That's wonderful" or "Thank you for sharing that with me" or "It's great that you love me" are likely to leave us feeling dissatisfied, exposed, foolish, vulnerable, even humiliated ("I told her that I love her and all she said was 'Thank you'!"). Anyone who's gone out on the "I love you" limb knows the special agony of waiting for the response. And anyone who's been on the receiving end without wanting to be knows how painfully awkward it is to feel obliged to reciprocate.

But, couldn't we just fake a response in order to satisfy the obligation to reciprocate? People do this all the time in other situations, as in "You look great today"; "Thanks, so do you." We certainly could fake it, but we do so at our peril because unlike "You look great, too," "I love you" is a powerful bit of performative language that amounts to far more than a simple exchange of compliments and other pleasant thoughts. In relationships that have a romantic potential (unlike, for example, the relationship between parents and children), saying "I love you" for the first time is far more than a way to make someone feel good. It is also an invitation and an expression of intent to alter a social relationship. If we reciprocate with "I love you, too," something happens immediately that changes our relationship to the other person. Suddenly the expectations and understandings that connect us shift. There might, for example, be an expectation of adding a sexual dimension to the relationship, a preference for and loyalty toward that person above everyone else in all kinds of situations. We might even be expected to form a long-term if not permanent relationship that involves living together or forming a family.

As performative language, the words do more than communicate; they also act on social reality and transform it by altering our relationship with someone else. They are "I do" on a less formally binding level and are important not simply for what they mean as for what they *do*. In this sense, all the positive feelings typically associated with "I love you" are, without the performative words themselves, merely information without transformation: "You say I'm wonderful, attractive, sexy, smart, and funny, that I excite you, interest you, and move you, and that you want to be with me; but you've never said you *love* me." The words are both crucial and powerful because they signal the crossing of a structural boundary around the love relationship. This is why we're so careful about when and with whom we say them. It's one thing to use just the word "love" as when signing a letter to a friend, but quite another to say "I love you." It's the difference between expressing a sentiment and declaring a relationship.

Using the words can take us across the boundary into a new relationship that radically alters our responsibilities and obligations. This difference between love as feeling and love as relationship is beautifully illustrated in the film *Harold and Maude*, in which a young and suicidally depressed Harold falls in love with the elderly, free-spirited Maude. Unbeknownst to Harold, Maude has a long-standing plan to end her life on her 70th birthday, having decided that this will be the right time for her to die. She takes a drug overdose and when Harold finds out he rushes her to the hospital. Desperate to save her, he protests that she can't do this because "I love you, Maude." But she won't join him in his definition of feeling as a binding relationship: "Wonderful!" she replies, "Go love some more!"

"I love you" works as performative language in many situations other than romantic ones, with quite different dynamics and results. When parents say "I love you" to their children, for example, it means something different than when children say the same words to their parents. This reflects a profound difference in the roles of parent and child. For the parent, the words typically convey not only loving feelings, but a commitment to the child's well-being. The words are so closely tied to that commitment that they may not tell children much about how the parent actually feels toward them, which is why children often make a distinction between being loved by their parents and being liked by them. The role relationship between parents and children requires that parents love them in the sense of being committed to their care; but it doesn't require that parents like them. From children's end of things, saying "I love you" may not have much to do with how they actually feel toward parents, especially when they're too young to know much about what love is. Instead, the words can be a way to elicit reassurance from parents that the relationship is sure and certain, as shown when the parent reciprocates with "I love you, too." This kind of ritual also works between adult partners as a short-hand way of signaling an ongoing commitment to the relationship.

The power of performative language requires us to use it with care. If we don't, we risk punishment reserved for people who show too little respect for its cultural authority and the harm its misuse can do. Nothing makes us unfit for social relationships as quickly as the habit of abusing performative language—the person who lies, who breaks promises, who dodges responsibility for injury and loss, or who professes love falsely or casually. In this sense, language is far more than talk, and we, in using it, are far more than mere talkers. We create and transform, spinning the world, ourselves, and one another as we speak.

Why Don't People
in the United States Vote?

I'm writing this a few days before election day. As I think about what I plan to do this Tuesday, I'm reminded that, if the past is any guide, millions of eligible voters probably won't join me in exercising their constitutional right. It's a puzzle, especially given how many billions of people have no right to vote in the first place, and even more of a puzzle when I consider that we're much less likely to vote than people are in Canada and most of Europe. What's going on? If I look at the question sociologically, I have to begin with the principle that voting and not voting are two ways to participate in a political system. Given this, I have to ask how the political system is organized so that not voting appears as a path of least resistance for millions of people. Can a political system that celebrates democratic principles actually discourage people from voting?

Yes, it can and does. I begin with the fact that it's hard to register as a voter in the United States. Registration is automatic in Canada, but in the United States you must apply in advance and be accepted as a voter. Recent laws make it possible to register as part of applying for a driver's license, but it still isn't a right that comes automatically with the fact of citizenship. Since a fairly high percentage of registered voters do vote, it's reasonable to assume that the easier it is to register, the more participation there will be. That the United States is so reluctant to make registration easy reflects a long-standing cultural bias against the lower classes, newly arrived immigrants, and others who might use political power to disturb the status quo and the privilege of dominant groups. In the years following the revolution for independence that launched the great American experiment in "democracy," for example, only white men who owned property were allowed to vote.

If we go deeper into the structure of the political system, we find that it's put together in ways that discourage people from registering or voting by taking away the potential for their vote to make a difference. Elections are organized on a winner-take-all principle. This means that in order to be represented in government, you must have a candidate who can win a majority of votes in a district. This makes it impossible for minority points of view to be represented in state or federal legislatures unless they can put together a majority across an entire district, which is hard to do. This appeared in a dramatic way in the decision to exclude third-party candidate Ross Perot from the 1996 presidential debates on the grounds that he didn't have a reasonable chance of winning a majority of the nation's votes.

In contrast to the United States, most European parliaments apportion seats according to the percentage of the vote each party receives. If your party wins five percent of the vote, your party gets five percent of the seats. But in the United States, a party could get as much as 49.99 percent of the vote without getting *any* seats at all. This means that if you support a candidate or party that cannot win a majority of all the votes in your district, it's easy to conclude that your vote won't make a difference. You might gain moral satisfaction from doing your civic duty, or protest by voting for "none of the above" or a candidate who shares your views but can't possibly win. But your vote cannot result in your views having representation in the government. European voters, however, can go to the polls knowing that each vote they cast will have a real additive effect that builds a political party's representation in the government.

Another reason that many people don't vote is that the U.S. political system is organized around just two major political parties. The Republicans and Democrats differ on some issues such as abortion rights and gun control, but they share an overall support for capitalism, wealth, property, and the use of military force to defend and advance national interests. They also share a willingness to abandon people living in poverty who depend on welfare; a tendency to use immigrants, people in the lower class, teenage mothers, and blacks as scapegoats for social problems; and a resistance to doing anything serious about problems like racism, sexism, and other forms of privilege and oppression. If you belong to one of the groups whose interests the major parties don't support, then it's easy to see the political system as loaded toward interests that aren't yours. From this perspective, it doesn't matter which party rules. It also doesn't matter whether you vote or not, for the outcome for you will be the same either way. In 1996, for example, the federal government drastically cut welfare benefits and turned away from its long-standing commitment to care for its neediest citizens, including children living in poverty. The law was passed by a Republican-controlled Congress and signed by a Democratic president.

In the 1990s, Republicans and Democrats joined in what Harvard economist John Kenneth Galbraith described as a "revolt of the contented against the unfortunate."[2] The United States has a political system controlled by a majority of the voting population who are content with the way things are: "It operates under the compelling cover of democracy, albeit a democracy not of all citizens but of those who, in defense of their social and economic advantage, actually go to the polls and vote. The result is a government accommodated not to reality or common need, but to the beliefs of the contented who are a majority of the actual voters."[3] It should come as no surprise, then, that you're more likely to vote if you're in the middle or upper classes, if you have a good job, or if you're white.

It's become a common practice to explain low voter turnout in terms of psychological conditions such as apathy. Sociologically, however, this misses the underlying fact that how people feel arises from their participation in social systems. When a political system is organized in ways that make staying away from the polls a rational choice for millions of people, it rings somewhat hollow to argue that citizens don't vote simply because "they don't care."

Why Is There Poverty? Putting the "Social" Back into Social Problems

Following the course of major social problems such as poverty, drug abuse, violence, and oppression, it often seems that nothing works. Government programs come and go; political parties swing us back and forth between stock answers whose only effect seems to be who gets elected. If anything, problems get worse, and people feel increasingly helpless and frustrated or, if the problems don't affect them personally, often feel nothing much at all. As a society, then, we are stuck, and we've been stuck for a long time.

One reason we're stuck is that the problems are huge and complex. But on a deeper level, we tend to think about them in ways that keep us from getting *at* their complexity in the first place. It is a basic tenet of sociological practice that to solve a social problem we have to begin by seeing it as social.[4] Without this, we look in the wrong place for explanations and in the wrong direction for visions of change.

Consider, for example, poverty, which is arguably the most far-reaching, long-standing cause of chronic suffering there is. The magnitude of poverty is especially ironic in a country like the United States whose enormous wealth dwarfs that of entire continents. Roughly one out of every five people in the United States lives in poverty or near-poverty. For children, the rate is even higher.[5] Even in the middle class there is a great deal of anxiety about the possibility of falling into poverty or something close to it—through divorce, for example, or simply being laid off as companies try to improve their competitive advantage, profit margins, and stock prices.

How can there be so much misery and insecurity in the midst of such abundance? If we look at the question sociologically, one of the first things we see is that poverty doesn't exist all by itself. It is simply one end of an overall distribution of income and wealth in society as a whole. As such, it is both a structural aspect of the system and an ongoing consequence of how the system is organized and the paths of least resistance that shape how people participate in it. The system we have for producing and distributing wealth is capitalist. It is organized in ways that allow a small elite to control most of the capital—factories, machinery, tools—used to produce wealth. This encourages the accumulation of wealth and income by the elite and regularly makes heros of those who are most successful at it—such as Microsoft's Bill Gates. It also leaves a relatively small portion of the total of income and wealth to be divided among the rest of the population. With a majority of the people competing over what's left to them by the elite, it's inevitable that a substantial number of people are going to wind up on the short end and live in poverty or the fear of it at least some of the time. It's like the game of musical chairs: Since the game is set up with fewer chairs than there are people, someone *has* to wind up without a place to sit when the music stops.

In part, then, poverty exists because the economic system is organized in ways that encourage the accumulation of wealth at one end and make poverty inevitable at the other. But the capitalist system generates poverty in other ways as well. In the drive for profit, for example, capitalism places a high value on competition and efficiency. This motivates companies and their managers to control costs by keeping wages as low as possible and replacing people with machines or replacing full-time workers with part-time workers. It makes it a rational choice to move jobs to regions or countries where labor is cheaper and workers are less likely to complain about poor working conditions, or where laws protecting the natural environment from industrial pollution or workers from injuries on the job are weak or unenforced. Capitalism encourages owners to shut down factories and invest money elsewhere in enterprises that offer a higher rate of return. These kinds of decisions are a normal consequence of how capitalism operates as a system; they are paths of least resistance that managers and investors are rewarded for following. But the decisions also have terrible effects on millions of people and their communities. Even having a full-time job is no guarantee of a decent living, which is why so many families depend on the earnings of two or more adults just to make ends meet. All of this is made possible by the simple fact that in a capitalist system most people neither own nor control any means of producing a living without working for someone else.

To these social factors we can add others. A high divorce rate, for example, results in large numbers of single-parent families who have a hard time depending on a single adult for both child-care and a living income. The centuries-old legacy of racism in the United States continues to hobble millions of people through poor education, isolation in urban ghettos, prejudice, discrimination, and the disappearance of industrial jobs that, while requiring relatively little formal education, nonetheless once paid a decent wage. These were the jobs that enabled many generations of white European immigrants to climb out of poverty, but which are now unavailable to the masses of urban poor.[6]

Clearly, patterns of widespread poverty are inevitable in an economic system that sets the terms for how wealth is produced and distributed. If we're interested in doing something about poverty itself—if we want a society largely free of impoverished citizens—then we'll have to do something about both the system people participate in and how they participate in it. But public debate about poverty and policies to deal with it focus almost entirely on the latter with almost nothing to say about the former. What generally passes for "liberal" and "conservative" approaches to poverty are, in fact, two variations on the same narrow theme of individualism.

A classic example of the conservative approach is Charles Murray's book *Losing Ground.*[7] Murray sees the world as a merry-go-round. The goal is to make sure that "everyone has a reasonably equal chance at the brass ring—or at least a reasonably equal chance to get on the merry-go-round."[8] He reviews thirty years of federal antipoverty programs and notes that they've generally failed. He concludes from this that since government programs haven't worked, poverty must not be caused by social factors. Instead, it's caused by failures of individual initiative and effort. People are poor because there's something lacking in them, and changing them is therefore the only effective remedy. From this he suggests doing away with public solutions such as affirmative action, welfare, and income support systems, including "AFDC, Medicaid, food stamps, unemployment insurance, and the rest. It would leave the working-aged person with no recourse whatsoever except the job market, family members, friends, and public or private locally funded services."⁹ The result, he believes, would "make it possible to get as far as one can go on one's merit."¹⁰ With the 1996 welfare reform act, the United States took a giant step in Murray's direction by reaffirming its long-standing cultural commitment to individualistic thinking and the mass of confusion around alternatives to it.

The confusion is about how we think about individuals and society and about poverty as an individual condition and as a social problem. On the one hand, we can ask how individuals are sorted into different social class categories. What characteristics best predict who will get ahead, who will get the best jobs and earn the highest incomes? If you want to get ahead, what's your best strategy? Based on many people's experience, the answers come fast and easy: work hard, get an education, don't give up when the going gets rough. There is certainly a lot of truth in this advice, and it gets to the issue of how people choose to participate in the system as it is. Sociologically, however, it focuses on only one part of the equation by leaving out the system itself. In other words, it ignores the fact that social life is shaped *both* by the nature of systems *and* how people participate, by the forest *and* the trees. Changing how individuals participate may affect outcomes for some. As odd as this may seem, however, this has relatively little to do with the larger question of why widespread poverty exists at all as a social phenomenon.

Imagine for a moment that income is distributed according to the results of a footrace. All of the income in the United States for each year is put into a giant pool and we hold a race to determine who gets what. The fastest fifth of the population gets 45 percent of the income to divide up; the next fastest fifth splits 25 percent; the next fastest fifth gets 15 percent; the next fifth 10 percent; and the slowest fifth divides 5 percent. The result would be an unequal distribution of income, with each person in the fastest fifth getting nine times as much money as each person in the slowest fifth. It would look roughly like the actual distribution of income in the United States.

If we look at the slowest fifth of the population and ask, "Why are they poor?" an obvious answer is, "They didn't run as fast as everyone else, and if they ran faster, they'd do better." This prompts us to ask why some people run faster than others, and to consider all kinds of answers from genetics to nutrition to motivation to having time to work out to being able to afford a personal trainer. But to see why *some* fifth of the population *must* be poor no matter how fast people run, all we have to do is look at the system itself. It uses unbridled competition to determine not only who gets fancy cars and nice houses, but who gets to eat or has a place to live or access to health care. It distributes income and wealth in ways that promote increasing concentrations among those who already have the most. Given this, the people in this year's bottom fifth might run faster next year and get someone else to take their place in the bottom fifth. But there *has* to be a bottom fifth so long as the system is organized as it is. Learning to run faster may keep you or me out of poverty, but it won't get rid of poverty itself. To do that, we have to change the system along with how people participate in it. Instead of splitting the "winnings" into shares of 45 percent, 25 percent, 15 percent, 10 percent, and 5 percent, for example, we might divide them into shares of 24 percent, 22 percent, 20 percent, 18 percent, and 16 percent. There would still be inequality, but the fastest fifth would get only 1.5 times as much as the bottom instead of 9 times as much, and 1.2 times as much as the middle fifth rather than 3 times as much.

People can argue about whether chronic widespread poverty is morally acceptable or what an acceptable level of inequality might look like. But if we want to understand where poverty comes from, what makes it such a stubborn feature of social life, we have to begin with the simple sociological fact that patterns of inequality result as much from how social systems are organized as they do from how individuals participate in them. Focusing on one without the other simply won't do it.

The focus on individuals is so entrenched, however, that even those who think they're taking social factors into account usually aren't. This is as true of Murray's critics as it is of Murray himself. Perhaps Murray's greatest single mistake is to misinterpret the failure of federal antipoverty programs. He assumes that federal programs actually target the social causes of poverty, which means that if they don't work, social causes must not be the issue. But he's simply got it wrong. Welfare and other antipoverty programs are "social" only in the sense that they're organized around the idea that social systems like government have a responsibility to do something about poverty. But antipoverty programs are *not* organized around a sociological understanding of how systems *produce* poverty in the first place. As a result, they focus almost entirely on changing individuals and not systems, and they use the resources of government and other systems to make it happen. If antipoverty programs have failed, it isn't because the idea that poverty is socially caused is wrong. They've failed because policymakers who design them don't understand what makes a cause "social." Or they understand it but don't act on it by targeting systems such as the economy for serious change. They're as trapped in individualistic thinking as everyone else in this culture.

The easiest way to see this is to look at the antipoverty programs themselves. They come in two main varieties. The first holds individuals responsible by assuming that financial success is solely a matter of individual qualifications and behavior. In other words, if you just run faster, you'll finish the race ahead of people who are currently beating you, and then *they'll* be poor instead of you. We get people to run faster by providing training and motivation. What we don't do, however, is look at the rules of the race or question whether the basic necessities of life should be distributed through competition. The result is that some people rise out of poverty by improving their competitive advantage, while others sink into it when their advantages no longer work and they get laid off or their company relocates to another country or gets swallowed up in a merger that boosts the stock price for shareholders and earns the CEO a salary that averages twenty-five times what the average employee receives. But nothing is even said—much less done—about an economic system that allows a small elite to own and control most of the wealth and sets up the rest of the population to compete over what's left. And so, individuals rise and fall in the class system, and the stories of those who rise are offered as proof of what's possible, and the stories of those who fall are offered as caution-ary tales. The system itself, however, including the huge gap be-tween the wealthy and everyone else and the steady proportion of people living in poverty, stays much the same.

A second type of program seems to assume that individuals aren't to blame for their impoverished circumstances, because it reaches out with various kinds of direct aid that help people meet day-to-day needs. Welfare payments, food stamps, housing subsidies, and Medicaid all soften poverty's impact; but they don't do anything about the steady supply of people living in poverty. There's nothing wrong with this in that it can alleviate a lot of suffering. But it shouldn't be confused with solutions to poverty, no more than army hospitals can stop wars. In relation to poverty as a social problem, welfare and other such programs are like doctors who keep giving bleeding patients transfusions without repairing the wounds. In effect, Murray tells us that fed-eral programs just throw good blood after bad. In a sense, he's right, but not for the reasons he offers. Murray would merely substitute one ineffective individualistic solution for another. If we do as he suggests and throw people on their own, certainly some will find a way to run faster than they did before. But that won't do anything about the "race" or the overall patterns of in-equality that result from using it as a way to organize one of the most important aspects of social life.

Liberals and conservatives are locked in a tug of war between two individualistic solutions to problems that are only partly about individuals. Both approaches rest on profound misunder-standings of what makes a problem like poverty "social." Neither is informed by a sense of how social life actually works as a dy-namic relation between social systems and how people participate in those systems. This is also what traps them between blaming problems like poverty on individuals and blaming them on society. Solving social problems doesn't require us to choose or blame one or the other. It does require us to see how the two combine to shape the terms of social life and how people actually live it.

Because social problems are more than an accumulation of individual woes, they can't be solved through an accumulation of individual solutions. We must include social solutions that take into account how economic and other systems really work. We also have to identify the paths of least resistance that produce the same patterns and problems year after year. This means that capitalism can no longer occupy its near-sacred status that holds it immune from criticism. It may mean that capitalism is in some ways incompatible with a just society in which the well-being of some does not require the misery of so many others. It won't be easy to face up to such possibilities, but if we don't, we will guarantee poverty its future and all the conflict and suffering that goes with it.

Who Are We Really?

Since people are the ones who make social life happen, sociological practice can't help but take me back to myself from time to time. It's one thing to think about issues like social oppression as "big" problems, for example, but quite another to see what they've got to do with me.

On a cool spring evening some years ago, I took a walk down a street I lived on in a small university town. Darkness was just coming on and there were just a few people on the street. As I walked along, I approached a young woman walking in the opposite direction. I'd never seen her before, but as we drew near I sensed something that startled and perplexed me. And, as my vivid memory of that moment shows, it still troubles me decades later. As we passed each other, she dropped her head, averted her eyes, quickened her step, and veered just a little to one side to widen the gap between us. She seemed to shrink in her body as if to take up less space. She was, I realized suddenly, afraid of me, walking down this peaceful street on this lovely evening. Afraid of me, who hadn't the slightest inclination to do her any harm.

But her reaction had nothing to do with what I intended; it had to do simply with my membership in a social category of people—adult males—who are the source of most of the world's violence and all of the harassment directed at women. That was all she knew about me, and yet this was enough to stir up fear and deference as she moved to hand the sidewalk over to me at that instant of our passing. That isn't what I wanted, but it didn't matter what I wanted, which is the sociological point of the story and the core of my dilemma as an individual.

Social life produces all kinds of consequences, including paths of least resistance that shape how we perceive and think about one another, how we feel, what we do. We aren't the paths; they exist in a given situation regardless of whether we know about them or whether they lead where we'd most like to go. That I've never been sexually harassing or violent is sociologically irrelevant, because the power and threat that she associated with "adult male" are rooted in a male-dominated, male-identified, and male-centered world in which we both participated. Since there is no "typical" violent or harassing male, there was nothing about me that marked me as a dangerous individual, but there was also nothing about me that could assure her that I wasn't. The same was true for her as a potential target since the characteristic that victims of sexual harassment and violence have most in common is the simple fact of being female. In short, in this kind of society, my being male was enough to mark me as a threat, and her being female was enough for her to feel vulnerable to being singled out for sexual harassment and violence.

When I realized what was going on, my first reaction was to defend myself. After all, I'm not one of *them*, I thought. I'm me, Allan, not just a member of some social category. In a sense, of course, I was right; but in another sense, I was quite wrong. My struggle and confusion were over what to make of these categories I belong to, which are most of what many people ever know of me, and certainly all that young woman could know at that moment. What I came to realize still later was that my insistence on being treated as an individual separate from my place in social systems was a luxury that I could afford in part because of the privileges attached to those same positions. Like many white men, I didn't want to think about race or gender, about my being male and white as significant and problematic in a sexist and racist world. Because if I did, I'd have to rethink my comfortable assumptions about how my life was connected to other people's lives through the systems we all participate in.

When white men complain about affirmative action programs, for example, they tend to draw attention to issues of individual merit.[11] They are very aware of their own talents and hard work and want to attribute what they get and what they deserve solely to that. What they ignore are the social advantages they have over women and racial minorities who are just as talented and work just as hard as they do. They ignore the fact that their success depends in part on competition limited by barriers routinely placed in front of other groups. Women and blacks, for example, are surrounded by a culture that makes them invisible, that offers little encouragement and support in school, and, when all else fails, openly discriminates against them. And the white male advantage is so built into the structure of systems that it doesn't even require open and deliberate discrimination. In most corporations, for example, the only way to get ahead is to have someone above you notice your potential and act as your mentor and sponsor.[12] Most mentors and sponsors tend to select those they feel most "comfortable" with—meaning those who are most like them. Since most people who are in a high enough position to offer mentoring are white males, the path of least resistance is to select other white males to bring along. As long as the promotion process is organized in this way, the advantages that white males enjoy will continue, *even though they typically don't experience them as such*. They'll be aware of how hard they've worked to get ahead, so that when a program like affirmative action comes along, they'll cry foul at the "unfair advantages" being given to others. What they don't see are the unfair advantages that are so deeply embedded in how the system is organized that they don't stand out as advantages at all, but simply the way things are.

It's hard to sort out who we are in relation to the statuses we occupy, to get a clear sense of some "real me" that participates in social systems but isn't *just* a participant in systems, and this is especially true in societies that place a high value on individualism. We certainly are more than status occupants and role players, but from the moment we're born, just about everything we experience is so entwined with one system or another that the distinction between us and our statuses and roles is hard to make. I believe, for example, that I have a soul, and that my soul is not a social creation. But the belief itself and all the ways I have available for *thinking* about "soul" are rooted in one culture or another. In moments of spiritual practice, I may have experiences that seem separate from the world and social life. I can have moments in which I stop thinking altogether and sense a reality that seems deeper than words, deeper than thought shaped by culture and social experience. But such moments are few and far between, and although they remind me that there's more to human existence than what we know as social life, their fleeting nature also reminds me that social life is what my life is about most of the time.

When that young woman and I passed each other on the street, whatever fear she felt was based on my status as a man in relation to her status as a woman in a world that relates those statuses to each other in particular ways. It was based on a social reality that doesn't fit many of the ideas I have about myself or how I experience myself. But this doesn't mean that she was reacting to something unreal that didn't exist, because the social reality she and I participated in was every bit as real as the "real me" and the "real her." Neither of us created that reality, and as individuals there wasn't much we could do to change it all by ourselves. But it was, whether we liked it or not, connected to who we were in that moment and how we saw and acted in relation to each other.

In this way, sociological practice draws us repeatedly to the fact that everything is connected to everything else in one way or another. No experience, no action is complete unto itself; everything is fundamentally relational. The global economy isn't just about nations and flows of capital, it's also about communities and neighborhoods and job prospects and stress and arguments over family dinner tables. A large-scale problem like poverty isn't simply about how individuals choose to live; it's also about the systems they participate in that shape the alternatives from which they choose and the paths of least resistance they are encouraged to follow. And something as simple and unremarkable as two people passing on a sidewalk or having a conversation turns out to be far from simple, for it, too, happens in relation to a larger context that shapes its course and gives it meaning.

At every level of social life, the practice takes us toward a fuller understanding of what's going on and why we feel and act as we do. It provides a foundation for a deeper and clearer awareness of how our lives are connected to these "things larger than ourselves." All of this can enrich our lives and make them more interesting. But the promise of sociology is much greater than that as the ability to see how social life works becomes a routine part of *how* it works, as sociological thinking becomes a pervasive part of culture itself. It then becomes a powerful collective tool in the struggle to understand and do something about the problems that cause so much unnecessary suffering in the world. It empowers us to look at how we participate in social life and see ways to take some small share of responsibility for the consequences social life produces. It gives us a way to be not simply part of the problem, but also part of the solution. The world and we could not help but be better for it.

Notes

NOTES TO CHAPTER ONE

1. For some basics on diversity in the workplace, see Katharine Esty, Richard Griffin, and Marcie Schorr Hirsch, *Workplace Diversity* (Holbrook, MA: Adams, 1995); Brian McNaught, *Gay Issues in the Workplace* (New York: St. Martin's Press, 1993); and R. Roosevelt Thomas Jr., *Beyond Race and Gender* (New York: AMACOM, 1991).
2. For a classic article on the nature of privilege, see Peggy McIntosh, "White Privilege and Male Privilege," in *Gender Basics: Feminist Perspectives on Women and Men*, ed. Anne Minas (Belmont, CA: Wadsworth, 1993), 30–38.
3. There are of course numerous examples of cultures and historical periods where families have behaved in this way, especially in relation to daughters. But in places like the United States where organizations are routinely likened to families, this is not how normal family life is viewed.
4. For more on the concept of role conflict, see Erving Goffman, *Encounters* (Indianapolis: Bobbs-Merrill, 1961); Robert K. Merton, *Social Theory and Social Structure*, enlarged ed. (New York: Free

Press, 1968); and David A. Snow and Leon Anderson, "Identity Work among the Homeless: The Verbal Construction and Avowal of Personal Identities," *American Journal of Sociology* 92, 6 (1987): 1336–1371.

5. For a comprehensive summary of findings about the causes of suicide, see David Lester, *Why People Kill Themselves*, 3rd ed. (Springfield, IL: Charles C. Thomas, 1992).

6. U.S. Bureau of the Census, *Statistical Abstract of the United States: 1996* (Washington, DC: U.S. Government Printing Office, 1996).

7. For more on this way of looking at racism, see David T. Wellman, *Portraits of White Racism*, 2nd ed. (New York: Cambridge University Press, 1993).

8. See, for example, Ellis Cose, *The Rage of a Privileged Class* (New York: HarperCollins, 1993); Joe R. Feagin, "The Continuing Significance of Race: Antiblack Discrimination in Public Places," *American Sociological Review* 56, 1 (1991): 101–116; and Joe R. Feagin and Melvin P. Sikes, *Living with Racism: The Black Middle-Class Experience* (Boston: Beacon Press, 1994).

9. For useful perspectives on how white people can become more aware of how they're connected to a racist society on a personal level, see Paul Kivel, *Uprooting Racism: How White People Can Work for Racial Justice* (Philadelphia: New Society Publishers, 1996).

NOTES TO CHAPTER TWO

1. Susanne K. Langer, "The Growing Center of Knowledge," in *Philosophical Sketches* (Baltimore: Johns Hopkins University Press, 1962), 145–147. Emphasis in the original.

2. W. I. Thomas and Dorothy Swain Thomas, *The Child in America* (New York: Knopf, 1928), 572; Robert K. Merton, "The Sociology of Social Problems," in *Contemporary Social Problems*, 4th ed., eds. Robert K. Merton and Robert Nisbet (New York: Harcourt Brace Jovanovich, 1976), 22.

3. For sociological critiques of capitalism, just about any text in social stratification will do. See, for example, Harold R. Kerbo, *Social*

Stratification and Inequality: Class Conflict in the United States, 3rd ed. (New York: McGraw-Hill, 1996); and Richard C. Edwards, Michael Reich, and Thomas E. Weisskopf, eds., *The Capitalist System,* 3rd ed. (Englewood Cliffs, NJ: Prentice-Hall, 1986).

4. See James L. Spates, "The Sociology of Values," *Annual Review of Sociology* 9 (1983): 27–49.

5. Quoted in Marvin Harris, *Cultural Materialism* (New York: Random House, 1979), 60.

6. Roger Brown, *Social Psychology* (New York: Free Press, 1965), 407.

7. Émile Durkheim, *Sociology and Philosophy* (New York: Free Press, 1974 [first published in 1924]).

8. See Erving Goffman, *Stigma: Notes on the Management of a Spoiled Identity* (Englewood Cliffs, NJ: Prentice-Hall, 1963).

9. See, for example, Edwin M. Schur, *Labeling Women Deviant: Gender, Stigma, and Social Control* (New York: Random House, 1984).

10. See, for example, Marilyn French, *Beyond Power: On Men, Women, and Morals* (New York: Summit Books, 1985); Carol Brooks Gardner, *Passing By: Gender and Public Harassment* (Berkeley: University of California Press, 1995); and National Council for Research on Women, *Sexual Harassment: Research and Resources,* 3rd ed. (New York: National Council for Research on Women, 1995).

11. Lawrence Mishel and Jared Bertsein, *The State of Working America: 1992–1993* (Armonk, NY: M. E. Sharpe for Economic Policy Institute, 1993); United Nations figures reported in the *Los Angeles Times, World Report,* 14 June 1994.

12. See Gordon W. Allport, "Attitudes," in *A Handbook of Social Psychology,* ed. Charles Murchison (Worcester, MA: Clark University Press, 1935); and K. J. Keicolt, "Recent Developments in Attitudes and Social Structure," *Annual Review of Sociology* 14 (1988): 381–403.

13. See, for example, Henry Abelove, Michele Aina Barale, and David M. Halperin, eds., *The Lesbian and Gay Studies Reader* (New York: Routledge, 1993); Michael S. Kimmel and Michael A. Messner, eds., *Men's Lives,* 3rd ed. (New York: Macmillan, 1995); and Suzanne Pharr, *Homophobia: A Weapon of Sexism* (Inverness, CA: Chardon Press, 1988).

14. *New York Times*, 24 April 1983.
15. Michael Parenti, *Inventing Reality*, 2nd ed. (New York: St. Martin's Press, 1993), chapter 2.
16. *The Hartford (Conn.) Courant*, 2 April 1989, sec. G1.
17. See Juliet B. Schor, *The Overworked American: The Unexpected Decline of Leisure* (New York: Basic Books, 1993).
18. Langer, "Growing Center of Knowledge," 147.

NOTES TO CHAPTER THREE

1. For more on the social significance of time, see R. H. Lauer, *Temporal Man: The Meaning and Uses of Social Time* (New York: Praeger, 1981); Pitirim A. Sorokin and Robert K. Merton, "Social Time: A Methodological and Functional Analysis," *American Journal of Sociology* 42 (1937): 615–629; Eviatar Zerubavel, *Hidden Rhythms: Schedules and Calendars in Social Life* (Chicago: University of Chicago Press, 1981); and Eviatar Zerubavel, *The Seven-Day Week: The History and Meaning of the Week* (New York: Free Press, 1985).
2. For the classic statement on the concept of social structure, see Robert K. Merton, *Social Theory and Social Structure*, enlarged ed. (New York: Free Press, 1968).
3. See Jerold Heiss, "Social Roles," in *Social Psychology: Sociological Perspectives*, ed. Morris Rosenberg and Ralph H. Turner (New York: Basic Books, 1981); and, for the classic statement on the subject, Ralph Linton, *The Study of Man* (New York: Appleton-Century-Crofts, 1936).
4. This, of course, can also happen between female teachers and male students or between teachers and students of the same sex. But the problems that are the focus of this discussion overwhelmingly occur between male teachers in positions of authority and females who are subordinate to them in some way. See, for example, Michele A. Paludi and L. A. Strayer, *Ivory Power: Sexual Harassment on Campus* (Albany: State University of New York Press, 1990); Center for Research on Women, *Secrets in Public: Sexual Harassment in Our Schools* (Wellesley, MA: Wellesley College Center for

Research on Women, 1993); Billie Wright Dziech and Linda Weiner, *The Lecherous Professor: Sexual Harassment on Campus* (Boston: Beacon Press, 1984).

5. See, for example, Joan Abramson, *Old Boys—New Women: Sexual Harassment in the Workplace* (New York: Praeger, 1993); Carol Brooks Gardner, *Passing By: Gender and Public Harassment* (Berkeley: University of California Press, 1995); Barbara A. Gutek, *Sex and the Workplace: The Impact of Sexual Behavior and Harassment on Women, Men, and Organizations* (San Francisco: Jossey-Bass, 1985); Catharine A. MacKinnon, *Sexual Harassment of Working Women: A Case of Sex Discrimination* (New Haven, CT: Yale University Press, 1979); Center for Research on Women, *Secrets in Public*; Dziech and Weiner, *The Lecherous Professor*; and Paludi and Strayer, *Ivory Power.*

6. See, for example, Susan Brownmiller, *Against Our Will: Men, Women, and Rape* (New York: Simon and Schuster, 1975); David Finkelhor and Kersti Yllo, *License to Rape: Sexual Abuse of Wives* (New York: Holt, Rinehart, and Winston, 1985); Michael A. Messner and Donald F. Sabo, *Sex, Violence, and Power in Sports: Rethinking Masculinity* (Freedom, CA: Crossing Press, 1994); Myriam Miedzian, *Boys Will Be Boys: Breaking the Link between Violence and Masculinity* (New York: Doubleday, 1991); Diana E. H. Russell, *Sexual Exploitation: Rape, Child Sexual Abuse, and Workplace Harassment* (Beverly Hills, CA: Sage, 1984); Peggy Reeves Sanday, *A Woman Scorned: Acquaintance Rape on Trial* (New York: Doubleday, 1996); and Patricia Searles and Ronald J. Berger, eds., *Rape and Society* (Boulder, CO: Westview Press, 1995).

7. Robert K. Merton, "Social Structure and Anomie," *American Sociological Review* 3 (1938): 672–682.

8. D. Jacobs, "Inequality and Economic Crime," *Sociology and Social Research* 66, 1 (1981): 12–28.

9. For more on this topic, see Carl N. Degler, *At Odds: Women and the Family in America from the Revolution to the Present* (New York: Oxford University Press, 1980); Robert L. Griswold, *Fatherhood in America: A History* (New York: Basic Books, 1993); and Eli Zaretsky, *Capitalism, the Family, and Personal Life*, revised and expanded ed. (New York: Harper and Row, 1986).

10. See Heidi Hartmann, "The Unhappy Marriage of Marxism and Feminism: Towards a More Progressive Union," in *Women and Revolution: A Discussion of the Unhappy Marriage of Marxism and Feminism*, ed. Lydia Sargent (Boston: South End Press, 1981), 1–41; and Martha May, "Bread before Roses: American Workingmen, Labor Unions, and the Family Wage," in *Women, Work, and Protest*, ed. Ruth Milkman (Boston: Routledge and Kegan Paul, 1985).

11. See Viviana A. Zelizer, *Pricing the Priceless Child: The Changing Social Value of Children* (New York: Basic Books, 1985).

12. Margaret Mead, *Coming of Age in Samoa* (New York: Modern Library, 1953 [first published in 1928]).

13. See E. Anthony Rotundo, *American Manhood: Transformations in Masculinity from the Revolution to the Modern Era* (New York: Basic Books, 1993).

14. U.S. Bureau of the Census, *Statistical Abstract of the United States: 1996* (Washington, DC: U.S. Government Printing Office, 1996).

15. For a clear look at racism as both cultural and structural, see David T. Wellman, *Portraits of White Racism*, 2nd ed. (New York: Cambridge University Press, 1993).

16. See Reynolds Farley and William H. Frey, "Changes in the Segregation of Whites from Blacks during the 1980s," *American Sociological Review* 59 (1994); Douglas S. Massey and Nancy A. Denton, *American Apartheid: Segregation and the Making of the Underclass* (Cambridge, MA: Harvard University Press, 1993).

17. See Lee Sigelman and S. Welch, "The Contact Hypothesis Revisited: Black-White Interaction and Positive Racial Attitudes," *Social Forces* 71, 3 (1993): 781–795.

18. Gunnar Myrdal, *An American Dilemma* (New York: Harper and Row, 1945).

19. Karl Marx, *Capital: A Critique of Political Economy* (New York: International Publisher, 1975 [first published in 1867]).

20. David R. Francis, "The Economic Expansion Is Finally Paying Off for Most Americans," *The Christian Science Monitor*, World Wide Web edition [www.csmonitor.com], 27 September 1996.

NOTES TO CHAPTER FOUR

1. For some basic statements, see Amos H. Hawley, *Human Ecology: A Theoretical Essay* (Chicago: University of Chicago Press, 1986); and Michael Micklin and Harvey M. Choldin, eds., *Sociological Human Ecology: Contemporary Issues and Applications* (Boulder, CO: Westview Press, 1984).

2. Virginia Woolf, *A Room of One's Own* (New York: Harcourt Brace and World, 1929).

3. The classic work on the social uses of space is Robert Sommer, *Personal Space: The Behavioral Analysis of Design* (Englewood Cliffs, NJ: Prentice-Hall, 1969).

4. See Donald S. Massey and Nancy A. Denton, *American Apartheid: Segregation and the Making of the Underclass* (Cambridge, MA: Harvard University Press, 1993).

5. For a fascinating novel that examines human beings as an "exceptional" species, see Daniel Quinn, *Ishmael* (New York: Bantam, 1992).

6. Marvin Harris, *Cows, Pigs, Wars, and Witches* (New York: Random House, 1974). See also his *Cannibals and Kings: The Origins of Cultures* (New York: Random House, 1977); *Cultural Materialism* (New York: Random House, 1979); and *Good Things to Eat: Riddles of Food and Culture* (New York: Simon and Schuster, 1985). For an introduction to sociology that uses an ecological approach, see Gerhard E. Lenski, Jean Lenski, and Patrick Nolan, *Human Societies*, 7th ed. (New York: McGraw-Hill, 1995).

7. U.S. Bureau of the Census, *Statistical Abstract of the United States: 1996* (Washington, DC: U.S. Government Printing Office, 1996).

8. U.S. Bureau of the Census, reported in the *Hartford (Conn.) Courant*, 20 September 1992, sec. A1.

9. See Population Reference Bureau, *World Population Data Sheet: 1996* (Washington, DC: Population Reference Bureau, 1996).

10. See B. P. Dohrenwend and B. S. Dohrenwend, "Sex Differences in Psychiatric Disorders," *American Journal of Sociology* 81 (1976): 1447–1454; and Lois Verbrugge and D. L. Wingard, "Sex Differentials in Health and Mortality," *Women and Health* 12, 2 (1987).

11. From data gathered by the University of Chicago National Opinion Research Center, General Social Surveys, 1996.
12. U.S. Bureau of the Census, *Statistical Abstract: 1996.*
13. Ibid.
14. Ibid.
15. Ibid.

NOTES TO CHAPTER FIVE

1. See, for example, B. F. Skinner, *Beyond Freedom and Dignity* (New York: Knopf, 1971).
2. For more on the concept of the self, see D. H. Demo, "The Self-Concept over Time: Research Issues and Directions," *Annual Review of Sociology* 18 (1992): 303–326; and Morris Rosenberg, *Conceiving the Self* (New York: Basic Books, 1979).
3. George Herbert Mead, *Mind, Self, and Society* (Chicago: University of Chicago Press, 1934).
4. Erving Goffman, *Encounters* (Indianapolis: Bobbs-Merrill, 1961).
5. Significant others is a term first introduced by Harry Stack Sullivan, *The Interpersonal Theory of Psychiatry* (New York: Norton, 1953).
6. Charles Horton Cooley, *Life and the Student* (New York: Knopf, 1927).
7. Mead, *Mind, Self, and Society.*
8. See the following works by Erving Goffman, *The Presentation of Self in Everyday Life* (New York: Doubleday and Company, 1959); *Asylums* (New York: Anchor Books, 1961); *Behavior in Public Places* (New York: Free Press, 1963); *Stigma: Notes on the Management of a Spoiled Identity* (Englewood Cliffs, NJ: Prentice-Hall, 1963); *Interaction Ritual* (New York: Anchor Books, 1967); *Gender Advertisements* (New York: Harper Colophon, 1976); *Forms of Talk* (Philadelphia: University of Pennsylvania Press, 1981); and *Encounters.* See also Philip Manning, *Erving Goffman and Modern Sociology* (Stanford, CA; Stanford University Press, 1992).
9. Erving Goffman, "Embarassment and Social Organization," *American Journal of Sociology* 62 (1956–1957): 264–271.

10. The study of methods people use to sustain the reality of a particular situation is known as ethnomethodology (literally, people's methods). It is most closely associated with the work of Harold Garfinkel. See his *Studies in Ethnomethodology* (Englewood Cliffs, NJ: Prentice-Hall, 1967). See also J. Maxwell Atkinson and John Heritage, *Structures of Social Action: Studies in Conversation Analysis* (Cambridge, England: Cambridge University Press, 1984); R. A. Hilbert, "Ethnomethodology and the Micro-Macro-Order," *American Sociological Review* 55, 6 (1990): 794–808; and Eric Livingston, *Making Sense of Ethnomethodology* (London: Routledge and Kegan Paul, 1987).

11. See Goffman, *Interaction Ritual.*

12. See, for example, Deborah Tannen, *You Just Don't Understand: Women and Men in Conversation* (New York: William Morrow, 1990); and her *Talking Nine to Five* (New York: William Morrow, 1994).

13. Rosabeth Moss Kanter, *Men and Women of the Corporation* (New York: Basic Books, 1977).

14. See Brian McNaught, *Gay Issues in the Workplace* (New York: St. Martin's Press, 1993).

15. For more on the concept of privilege, see Peggy McIntosh, "White Privilege and Male Privilege," in *Gender Basics: Feminist Perspectives on Women and Men,* ed. Anne Minas (Belmont, CA: Wadsworth, 1993), 30–38.

16. Such stories abound in the experiences of people of color in the United States. See, for example, Lois Benjamin, *The Black Elite* (Chicago: Nelson-Hall, 1991); Ellis Cose, *The Rage of a Privileged Class* (New York: HarperCollins, 1993); Joe R. Feagin, "The Continuing Significance of Race: Antiblack Discrimination in Public Places," *American Sociological Review* 56, 1 (1991): 101–116; Joe R. Feagin and Melvin P. Sikes, *Living with Racism: The Black Middle-Class Experience* (Boston: Beacon Press, 1994); Joe R. Feagin, *White Racism: The Basics* (New York: Routledge, 1995); and his *The Agony of Education: Black Students at White Colleges and Universities* (New York: Routledge, 1996); and David T. Wellman, *Portraits of White Racism,* 2nd ed. (New York: Cambridge University Press, 1993).

NOTES TO CHAPTER SIX

1. For the classic statement on the norm of reciprocity, see Alvin W. Gouldner, "A Norm of Reciprocity: A Preliminary Statement," *American Sociological Review* 25 (1960): 161–178. See also Marcel Mauss, *The Gift* (New York: Free Press, 1954 [first published in 1925]). For more on exchange theory, see Peter M. Blau, *Exchange and Power in Social Life* (New York: Wiley, 1986); and K. S. Cook, ed., *Social Exchange Theory* (Newbury Park, CA: Sage, 1987).

2. John Kenneth Galbraith, "Why the Welfare State Is Here to Stay," interview by Nathan Gardells, *The National Times*, June 1996, 30.

3. Ibid.

4. For a classic statement of this principle, see Robert K. Merton, "The Sociology of Social Problems," in *Contemporary Social Problems*, 4th ed., eds. Robert K. Merton and Robert Nisbet (New York: Harcourt Brace Jovanovich, 1976), 5–43.

5. U.S. Bureau of the Census, *Statistical Abstract of the United States: 1996* (Washington, DC: U.S. Government Printing Office, 1966).

6. See William Julius Wilson, *When Work Disappears: The World of the New Urban Poor* (New York: Knopf, 1996).

7. Charles Murray, *Losing Ground* (New York: Basic Books, 1984).

8. Ibid., 221.

9. Ibid., 227–228.

10. Ibid., 233.

11. On affirmative action, see Paul Kivel, *Uprooting Racism: How White People Can Work for Racial Justice* (Philadelphia, PA: New Society, 1996), 172–179; Nicolaus Mills, ed., *Debating Affirmative Action* (New York: Dell, 1994); and David T. Wellman, *Portraits of White Racism*, 2nd ed. (New York: Cambridge University Press, 1993), 226–236.

12. See R. Roosevelt Thomas Jr., *Beyond Race and Gender* (New York: AMACOM, 1991).

Index

abuse in families, causes of, 89–91
achieved status, 85
action, 150
adolescence, as life stage, 104
Aesop's fables, 92
affirmative action, 187–188
age structure, 133–134
agricultural societies, 128
American Dilemma, An, 111
Amos and Andy, 15–16, 27
ascribed status, 85, 100–101
attitudes, cultural, 63–67, 86, 108
authenticity, of self, 153–154

behavior, 150
beliefs, cultural, 44–47, 62, 63, 86,
    108
boundaries: community, 117; and in-
    equality, 117; norms, deviance,
    and, 57, 58; performative language
    and, 171

Brown, Roger, 52
bureaucracy, 100, 130

capitalism: contradictions in,
    112–114; criticism of, 71–72; and
    families, 101–107; government
    and, 113–114; as mode of produc-
    tion, 129; poverty and, 177–178;
    racism and, 109; as a social system,
    31, 112–114
Canada, voting in, 173
childcare, as women's work, 103
children, in family role structures,
    102, 103–104
China: bureaucracy in, 130; energy
    consumption in, 138; status of
    women in, 99
cities, inner, crisis in, 116–117
civil rights movement, 111
Clinton, Bill, 84
coalitions, 133